FOREST
ADVENTURES

Foreword by
JOHN BLANEY

FEASTING ★ EXPLORATIONS ★ ESCAPADES ★ CRAFTING ★ GAMES ★ PLAYGROUNDS

MORE THAN **80** IDEAS
TO RECONNECT WITH
NATURE ALL YEAR ROUND

FOREST
ADVENTURES

**CLAIRE GILLMAN
& SAM MARTIN**

m

CONTENTS

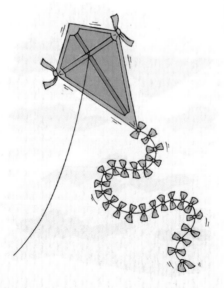

Every activity is graded for difficulty and shows the amount of time that you will need to complete it. One star symbol (★) indicates an acitivity that is simple to do, while three star projects will require helping hands and practise to get right.

FOREWORD
BY JOHN BLANEY

Education is one of the most important things we can give to children and, with my own love for the outdoors, it was always my passion to merge the two. In 1993 I had the opportunity to do so by creating the 'Forest School' concept, which supports children's education through the use of the outdoors for recreational, social and educational purposes. Fundamentally, Forest School is about using the natural world to ensure that children get to enjoy the outdoors while learning; it gives them a safe environment in which to experiment, develop and grow without fear of failure. All Forest School activities are adapted to meet a child's skill level, but also to allow them to progress as their confidence grows. I am delighted that my legacy of the Forest School has spread nationally and internationally, with thousands of children now enjoying the outdoors every week.

It is not only teachers who can use the Forest School concept to enhance the lives of children, but also parents, carers and other adults involved in their upbringing. At this time, when technology forms a major part of our children's lives, it has never been more important that children are taken outdoors to enjoy and learn about their environment.

Claire and Sam have produced this book packed with ideas that parents and carers can embrace and enjoy along with the children. The activities in this book will educate and enlighten children as they learn about the environment, from how to make a jam from seasonal berries, to how to identify animal tracks. The outdoor area you have available is not important as there are activities to suit any size of outdoor space, ranging from a bird feeder that could be hung on a balcony, to building a full-scale tree house. Whether you live in an urban, rural or coastal area, this book has something to suit all locations.

Going outdoors does not have to cost anything, and plenty of activities can be found in the book that do not cost a penny: children can go stargazing, take a walk and predict the weather, build a shelter in the woods and create beach art, to name just a few.

Parents and educators alike will find the ideas easy to understand and implement, and these activities will give them confidence in taking children outside. The activities vary in ability, for both the parents and children, from growing a sunflower and planning a picnic to building an igloo. Growing a sunflower or some herbs will teach children about how plants grow and what they need to survive, but it also teaches them patience and how to care for a living thing. It is only as they patiently nurture the seeds that they will reap the reward of a large colourful sunflower, or some herbs to add to a meal. Meanwhile, the homemade kite is an equally-valuable activity with a completely different set of skills, as this teaches children about shape, size and selecting the correct materials while also encouraging lots of physical activity when flying the kite. Any activity that encourages physical movement is wholeheartedly recommended by myself.

I particularly like the water escapades section as the beach changes every day and with the coming and going of the tide there is always something new to explore. This important environment can also be used to teach children about nature's diversity, conservation, recycling and it's power, such as the tides. The fabulous feasting section is great for any weather and the children can learn about which fruit is in season, how to follow a recipe and, of course, enjoy the end results of their hard work!

With such a wide range of activities on offer you will never be short of ideas for an outdoor adventure!

John Blaney introduced Forest Schools to the UK and teaches the Forest School concept internationally to inspire a love for learning in the outdoors.

1

OUTDOOR EXPLORATIONS

The great outdoors offers so much opportunity for fun and adventure. Whether you stay in your own garden to build a hideout or investigate the insect wildlife, or you venture further afield for hiking or camping, there's always plenty to do. You can even find out how to predict the weather, so you can avoid getting caught in a downpour while you're out!

READING A MAP

There's no greater sense of freedom than setting off on a day's adventure with your friends, armed only with a packed lunch and a map. But before you head off into the wild blue yonder, there are a few basic skills that you should get under your belt, like how to read a map.

SKILL LEVEL	★★
TIME NEEDED	1–2 hours

1 Find somewhere on the map that you want to travel to and make sure you know what your current position is on the map.

2 First, you'll notice that these kinds of maps have a grid of lines over the top of them as if someone was dividing them up into squares. The up-and-down lines are north and south. The left-to-right lines are east and west.

3 On some roadless maps you'll also notice lots of winding, curving lines. These are called contour lines and they tell you how the land drops off (for gorges or river beds) and rises up (for hills and mountains).

4 All maps have detailed legends or keys that will tell you what all the colours and lines mean. By referring to the key you can tell what kinds of trees, fields and rocks you can expect to find.

5 Put your compass on the map and line up the sides of the compass base plate with an imaginary line going from your present location to your destination. This means the direction arrow at the top of the compass base plate should be pointing in the direction of your destination.

YOU WILL NEED

A full-colour map

A compass

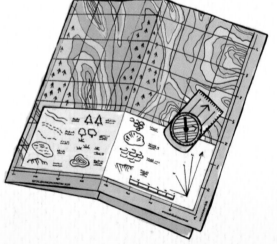

7 To reach your destination, walk in the direction of the arrow on the base plate while ensuring that the magnetic needle is aligned with the north arrow on the compass.

6 Without moving the compass base plate, rotate the central dial in the middle until its north arrow aligns itself with the compass's magnetic needle. This sets your bearing into the compass.

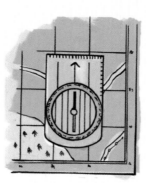

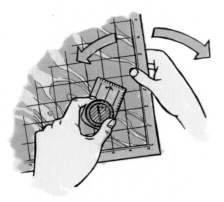

8 As you're walking, take note of your natural surroundings, like streams, buildings and areas of woodland. Then check to make sure they're on the map too by referring to the key, so you know you're on the right track. Don't forget to take regular bearings during your journey to also help keep you on track.

TOP TIP

Check the scale on the map when you plan your route – a 1:50,000 map scale means the map area is 50,000 times smaller than the real area; so a distance of 2.5 centimetres (1 inch) on the map is 125,000 centimetres (50,000 inches) or about 1.25 kilometres (0.8 miles).

FINDING NORTH

If you're planning any long hikes, you'll need to be able to find your way around. You should always have a map and compass with you so that you don't get lost, but if you want to add an additional challenge to your expedition, try finding your way north without using your compass. Many adventurers in history didn't have any instruments at all and they managed to complete their missions. You can too! You can find north using a few different methods without a compass.

SKILL LEVEL	★★
TIME NEEDED	5 minutes

USING A WATCH

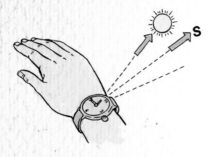

An analog watch can be made into a compass. Just hold it horizontal to the ground and point the hour hand directly at the sun. Then imagine a line running exactly in the middle between the hour hand and the 12 o'clock mark on your watch. That imaginary line points north and south – south being at the top of the line, which usually means you'll be facing south with north behind you.

If you're in the southern hemisphere point the watch's 12 o'clock mark in the direction of the sun and your north/south line will run between this and wherever the hour hand is. In this case, north is at the top of this line, meaning you'll probably be facing north with the southerly direction behind you.

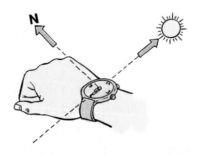

USING THE STARS

The ancient Polynesians of the South Pacific may have been history's best navigators. They discovered and settled thousands of islands with only their knowledge of the sky, passed down the generations through stories. Polynesian navigators, or Palus, were required to train for a long time before they could navigate their own ships. One part of the training was memorizing the colours of the sky and sea, the various clouds that would cluster over islands and the stars. Here's how to follow their example.

NORTHERN HEMISPHERE

1 Find the North Star, usually one of the brightest in the night sky, by first locating the Big Dipper. Draw an imaginary line joining the two stars that form the Big Dipper's front line and continue this line out about five times its original length. You should arrive at the North Star.

2 Now just draw an imaginary line from the North Star down to Earth. The star sits directly over the North Pole, so that way is north.

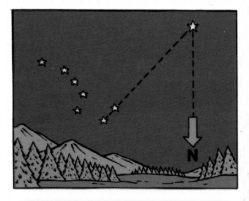

SOUTHERN HEMISPHERE

1 There is no North Star in the southern hemisphere. Instead, locate the constellation known as the Southern Cross, next to the constellation Centaurus.

2 Once you've picked out the four bright stars that form the Cross, look to the two stars that make the longer of the two crossbeams.

3 Extend this crossbeam out to five times its length and mark that imaginary point in the sky. A line drawn from that point down to Earth will give you an approximate south reading.

STARGAZING

Stargazing has been a human pastime since the beginning of time. Tracking constellations (groups of stars) was a way to mark the seasons for the Ancient Egyptians back in 2000 BC. Ptolemy, a Greek man who lived in Roman Egypt, was the first to name the constellations. Some of our Solar System's planets are visible to the naked eye — see if you can spot them.

SKILL LEVEL

SPOTTING PLANETS

Five of the planets are visible to the naked eye – Mercury, Venus, Mars, Jupiter and Saturn. Named after the Roman gods, they give us, together with the sun and the moon, the seven days of week. In China and Japan, the five planets are named after the five elements: Mercury is the water star, Venus is the metal star, Mars is the fire star, Jupiter is the wood star and Saturn is the earth star.

MERCURY Look for Mercury in the direction of the sunset about 45 minutes after the sun dips beneath the horizon, or in the direction of sunrise about 45 minutes before the sun comes up. The best times for viewing in the northern hemisphere are March and April (during sunset) and September and October (during sunrise). The opposite is true if you're planet-spotting in the southern hemisphere, where the best times to spot Mercury are sunrise in March and April, and sunset in September and October.

VENUS Venus is always the third-brightest object in the sky after the sun and moon, and is known alternately as the Morning or Evening Star. Venus can also be seen by looking in the direction of the setting or rising sun, and it is visible for much longer periods of time than Mercury.

MARS Mars is visible all night and is brightest every two years, when its orbit is closest to the Earth's and it is in opposition to our planet (the Earth is between it and the sun). The planet follows the same path as the sun across the night sky and is most visible looking east in the early morning. You can recognize it by its orange-red colour.

JUPITER Jupiter is the next brightest object in the sky after Venus – it's 1,300 times the volume of the Earth! It is best seen during twilight hours. If you have a telescope, you might be able to see Jupiter's large red spot.

SATURN Because Saturn is so far away (10 times further away from the sun than Earth), it's hard to see unless you know where to look. It's at its brightest when its rings are fully facing the Earth, but that only happens every 13 to 16 years. For now, look for a pale yellow star low in the western sky around dusk.

URANUS, NEPTUNE AND PLUTO

The three outermost planets in the Solar System are hard to see without a telescope. Pluto is now classified as a dwarf planet, much smaller than the others, and impossible to see with the naked eye.

CONSTELLATIONS

There are 88 different constellations mapped out all across the sky from Pole to Pole, east and west. The constellations you can see are different in the northern and southern hemispheres because the curve of the Earth hides some stars from us. You can look up star charts on the Internet or your local library which will tell you exactly where to look for constellations in different places and at different times of year. They can also tell you when to look for exciting events like meteor showers or a lunar eclipse! Star-spotting is best done away from cities as light pollution in urban areas makes it hard to see faint objects in the skies.

THE ZODIAC AND ASTROLOGY

The constellations of the zodiac can be found roughly along the path that the sun takes across the sky. Studied by human civilizations for thousands of years, they are called: Aries (the ram), Taurus (the bull), Gemini (the twins), Cancer (the crab), Leo (the lion), Virgo (the virgin), Libra (the scales), Scorpio (the scorpion), Sagittarius (the archer), Capricorn (the goat), Aquarius (the water-bearer) and Pisces (the fish). Each one has its own meanings and symbol. They are the basis for astrology, a system that many people believe can predict the future by the movements of the stars.

Each symbol is most visible at a particular time of year, and people born during that time are said to have characteristics of that symbol. Find your birthday on the list to see what star sign you are.

SIGNS OF THE ZODIAC

Aries: 21 March–20 April

Taurus: 21 April–21 May

Gemini: 22 May–21 June

Cancer: 22 June–23 July

Leo: 24 July–23 August

Virgo: 24 August–23 September

Libra: 24 September–23 October

Scorpio: 24 October–22 November

Sagittarius: 23 November–22 December

Capricorn: 23 December–20 January

Aquarius: 21 January–19 February

Pisces: 20 February–20 March

PREDICTING THE WEATHER

If you're planning an outdoors event like a picnic, or you've gone adventuring some distance from home, predicting the weather can be a very useful skill to have to avoid getting very wet. And it's also a good way to impress your fellow travellers.

SKILL LEVEL

CLOUD READING

There are four main types of clouds:

The highest-floating clouds – 5 kilometres (16,500 feet) or higher – are in the cirrus family. Cirrus clouds are wispy and static and do not indicate bad weather.

Clouds floating in the middle of the sky – 2 to 5 kilometres (6,500 to 16,500 feet) high – are known as alto clouds. They look like large patchy sheets that cover big parts of the sky. Seeing these on a warm day usually indicates thunderstorms later.

The lowest-floating clouds are stratus clouds. They can reach as high as 2 kilometres (6,500 feet), but can drop all the way to the surface of the planet as fog. While they don't always forecast rain, some of the types in this family do. Nimbostratus clouds, for example, look grey and fluffy while

covering the entire sky. Expect rain in the next few hours if you see these.

The last type of cloud is the vertical cloud, which can reach from ground level up to several kilometres high. These are the cumulus clouds, sometimes known as thunderheads. They are white, puffy and massive, and, as their name indicates, they forecast thunder, lightning and heavy rain or hail. If you see these rolling in, then watch out: a storm's brewing.

MAKING A WEATHER VANE

Another good method of predicting the weather is to know which way the wind is blowing, using a weather vane. Keep a log of the wind direction on rainy days and fine days and see if you can work out a pattern. If you know it always rains when the wind is in the southwest, you'll know what to expect the next time the wind blows from that direction.

SKILL LEVEL	★★
TIME NEEDED	15 minutes

1 Cut two pieces of plywood to make a triangle and a rectangle. Cut slits at each end of your piece of wood, and glue the plywood shapes into the slits to make a wooden arrow.

2 Hammer the nail through the centre of your arrow. Turn the nail a few times until the hole loosens so the arrow can spin freely.

3 Hammer the rest of the nail into the broom handle. Plant it securely in the ground in a windy spot and use a compass to tell which direction the arrow is pointing – that's where the wind is coming from!

YOU WILL NEED

Scrap pieces of plywood

A 30-cm (12-in) piece of wood

A saw (ask an adult for help to use this)

Wood glue

A hammer and a 7.5 cm (3 in) nail

A broom handle

MAKING A COMPASS

Invented in China over 1,000 years ago, compasses use the Earth's magnetic field indicate which way is north. Movement of lava beneath the Earth's crust creates a very weak magnetic field running between the planet's North and South Poles. A very light magnetic needle, if it's allowed to swing freely, will align itself with this field, because the poles on magnets attract and repel each other. This means the needle will always swing around to point north, no matter how you turn it.

Unfortunately, there are times we forget to pack a real compass, but not to worry – you can make one. Fortunately, the Earth's magnetic field is strong enough to attract magnetized sewing needles or paper clips if they're given freedom to spin by being floated on water. Here's how to set up your own so you can always tell which way is north.

SKILL LEVEL	★★
TIME NEEDED	15 minutes

YOU WILL NEED

A magnet

A small piece of metal, like a needle, paper clip or small nail

A plastic container to hold water

Water

A leaf or large blade of grass

1 Run the magnet slowly over the needle about ten times, making sure you do so in the same direction each time. This will make the needle magnetic enough to act as a compass.

2 If you don't have a magnet, you can still magnetize your needle or paper clip using static electricity. You can use material from a nylon raincoat or fleece jacket to build up the charge. Simply stroke the needle in the same direction with the material you have on hand. You need to do this at least 50 times.

3 Fill a plastic container with water and then gently place a leaf or large blade of grass on the water's surface, so it floats on top in the centre of the container.

4 Then carefully place the magnetized needle on top of the floating leaf or blade of grass, so that it floats freely on the surface of the water.

5 Watch as the needle will then turn to point itself towards the North Pole.

6 Try to test your homemade compass in a place that's sheltered from the wind. Earth's magnetic poles might be strong enough to attract a magnetized needle, but that doesn't say much. A breeze, even a gentle one, can easily push your leaf off course.

7 Of course, this will only show you a line between north and south. You need some other clues to work out which is which. The sun is one clue: in the northern hemisphere, the sun will always be in the southern half of the sky, on the eastern side in the morning and the western side in the evening. In the southern hemisphere, the sun will always be on the northern side of the sky.

REMEMBER!

This method won't work if you use a bowl made from metal to hold the water. The magnetized needle will be attracted to the metal bowl insead of swinging freely to point north.

DID YOU KNOW?

You've heard of north, south, east and west, but did you know old-time sailors divided the compass into 32 points? There are seven points between north and east: northeast is halfway between the two; north-northeast is halfway between north and northeast; north-by-east is halfway between north-northeast; and so on. A diagram showing all 32 points is called a 'compass rose'. Modern compasses are divided into 360 degrees, for even more accurate measurements.

HIKING

So, now you know which direction you're going in, but do you know how to get to your destination without blisters and still in high spirits? Well, here are a few tips on happy hiking. You need to be prepared for changeable weather conditions, so a backpack with an extra layer and some waterproof clothing is essential. You should also be able to find your way back home, so make sure you familiarize yourself with map reading before you set out on your adventure (see page 10).

(see page 10)

SKILL LEVEL	★★
TIME NEEDED	1 hour

1 Check the weather beforehand because it gives you a better idea of how to prepare.

2 It's a good idea at first to go with experienced hikers. If you don't have any hiking friends or family, join an organized group until you've got the hang of things – the local library is a good place to find details. Once you have some group hiking experience under your belt, you can start to go for longer and more challenging hikes.

3 Always wear comfortable clothes that are designed for the job. And don't worry that you'll look like a dork – there's some really great-looking outdoor gear available now. Take water and high-energy snacks with you. And don't forget the warm clothes.

4 Don't wear brand-new footwear on a hike or you'll end up with blisters. Wear your shoes in until they're comfortable and then start with short, easy hikes to get your muscles used to walking for when you do longer distances.

5 Plan your route together with your hiking group – something that you all agree is achievable.

6 Pack your kit: map, compass, water, energy snacks – and you're ready to go.

YOU WILL NEED

Outdoor clothing

Walking shoes or hiking boots

TRACKING

Your local wildlife will probably be most abundant in summer, when all the animals are out of their winter hibernation and their young are emerging from their nests and dens, so there should be plenty of tracks for you to find. Find out which animals live in your area and what you can expect to see (and what you should avoid). Tracking requires a powerful sense of awareness and observation. There are footprints to recognize, but that's the easy part. Skilled trackers also know how to find and follow all kinds of signs, symbols and clues, such as fur or feathers, broken sticks and leaves and animal scents and dung.

SKILL LEVEL	★ ★
TIME NEEDED	1–2 hours

HOW TO TRACK

Animals often use the same routes over and over, even if their territory covers hundreds of square miles. This makes things easier for the tracker – if you spot a well-used path, you can follow it to pick up the animal's trail. Of course, if the animal knows you're there, they'll likely change course or hide. That's why tracking takes plenty of practice and patience.

Take a look at the next page for a guide to tracking and identifying animal prints.

HOW TO TRACK ANIMALS

If you discover animal tracks, you'll want to know what kind of animal you're up against. Bears and large cats spell danger not adventure, so don't start following the trail if you spot their tracks. Deer, rabbits, and other small furry creatures are mostly harmless and it can be good fun to track them back to their lairs.

SKILL LEVEL

Scientists have been tracking the movements of birds and animals for centuries, and even they have had to learn on the job. In the old days, scientists would tie string markers to the legs of migrating birds to see if they would return to the same spot a year later (they often did). Now they attach radio tags to all kinds of animals – from elephants and big cats to whales and dolphins – to track their movements all over the world by satellite. Since most of us don't have access to electronic tags or satellites, we'll have to track like the primitive hunters in the old days. To follow an animal's trail, walk next to its prints, keeping the tracks between you and the sun so your shadow doesn't obscure them. Sometimes tracks can become faint, especially in drier weather, so try to spot additional signs like broken foliage, flattened grass or dung. Stay as quiet as you can. Talk in a whisper and avoid walking on dry twigs or leaves. Lastly, try to think like an animal – if you lose the trail in a natural boundary like a river or gorge, look for the easiest natural way forward. Follow your instincts until you catch up with the tracks again.

Often the tracks will stop at a burrow or watering place – if you wait there quietly (especially at dusk) there's a good chance you'll see your animal when it wakes up or decides it wants a drink. If you're lucky, and move quietly enough while you're tracking, you might catch up with whatever you're following, especially if it's stopping to graze or drink along the way. Then you can take a photo or just admire the creature – the best moment for any tracker.

HOW TO IDENTIFY ANIMAL PRINTS

Wild dogs like foxes and wolves always have diamond-shaped paws that are longer than they are wide. Plus, their prints have four toes tipped by claw marks. Big cats have retractable claws that won't show up in the mud (they also have four toes). Another characteristic of the big cats, like lions or jaguars, is that their toe marks are more circular than those of dogs. Bear prints have five toes with claw marks. They're also going to be significantly bigger than those of a fox or wildcat. Some examples of common animal prints are on the next page.

Wallaby

Wombat

Beaver

Cottontail rabbit

Crow

Dog

Black bear

Bobcat

Coyote

Grey squirrel

House cat

Moose

Muskrat

Possum

Otter

Raccoon

Porcupine

Red fox

Snowshoe hare

Turkey

Weasel

White-tailed deer

Mouse

COLLECTING WATER

A long day of hiking will surely make you thirsty, so you will need to find a water source. But, if you can't find one, you can always collect water for yourself during a storm or rain shower.

SKILL LEVEL	★
TIME NEEDED	30 minutes

1 Lay your plastic sheeting on the ground and mark out the points where the corners lie.

2 Push two long sticks into the ground at the back corners and two shorter sticks at the front corners. Drape the sheeting over the sticks so it sits off the ground and forms a slope.

3 Poke a small hole in the middle of the sheeting at the lower end. Tie a piece of string to this hole and tuck the other end under a heavy stone on the ground. This pulls the middle of the front of the sheet down to make a sort of spout, down which the collected rainwater will run.

4 Put a container under this spout and as soon as it rains, you'll have cold, running water.

YOU WILL NEED

Plastic sheeting

2 long, straight sticks

2 shorter sticks

String

A heavy stone

A container

TOP TIP

Rainwater harvesting has been around for thousands of years and was primarily used as a source of drinking water in rural areas. Free from pollutants, minerals and both natural and manmade contaminants, rainwater can be collected to water your garden – in fact, plants prefer rainwater to domestic water.

BUILDING A SHELTER

The elements themselves were the biggest danger faced by explorers. In addition to weatherproof clothing, they needed shelters to protect them from the wind, snow and cold temperatures. Here's a makeshift shelter you can make using natural materials, no matter what the weather is.

SKILL LEVEL	★★
TIME NEEDED	2 hours

1 First, find a large rock or tree stump and a sturdy branch to act as your ridge pole, which should be a metre (3 ft) or so taller than you. This will form the backbone of the shelter.

2 Brace your ridge pole firmly against the rock or tree stump. Find other sturdy sticks and branches, and tie them together with string to form two side supports. The tied ends of the sticks will be used to hold your ridge pole in place and the other ends will extend down to the ground. You will now have a tripod-like structure. It should be big enough to hold two explorers.

3 Line either side of the ridge pole with more sticks. After this, gather as much debris as you can find and thatch your whole shelter with it. Use whatever the surrounding area offers: leaves, pine needles, dried ferns, grass, mud, etc.

4 Real explorers kept a record of the things they saw so people could learn from their discoveries. While you are on your expedition, make notes about the weather, the animals and any difficulties you encountered along the way.

YOU WILL NEED

A large rock or tree stump

A sturdy branch for your ridge pole

Various sizes of branches and sticks

String

Debris

A notebook and pen

DID YOU KNOW?

The first explorer to reach the North Pole was American Navy engineer Robert Edwin Peary in 1909 – although he lost eight toes to frostbite during the attempt and was later dogged by claims that he didn't fully complete the journey to the Pole itself. Some believe a fellow American explorer, Dr Frederick Cook, reached the North Pole a year before Peary – and the controversy still lingers today.

BUILDING A HIDEOUT

You can use a hideout to watch for animals and birds. Or keep it as base camp for your adventures and as a place to store your adventuring supplies. Wherever you decide to build, seclusion is the key. It should be somewhere less travelled and not easily seen by the casual passerby.

SKILL LEVEL	★
TIME NEEDED	1 hour

FINDING A SITE You can set up your hideout anywhere you want – even inside, perhaps up in the attic, if a rainy day interrupts your adventure. Anywhere will do as long as you can find somewhere secluded. You could build one behind the shrubbery beside where you live, in a wood thicket, inside a thick patch of bushes or in a hollow tree in the woods.

CHOOSING YOUR MATERIALS All kinds of materials can be used, depending on where you want to build your hideout. If you're outdoors and want to be protected from the elements, try stringing up a tarpaulin between two trees. If you don't expect to see much rain, cardboard could be your material of choice. A collection of large boxes can be joined together with tape and you can cut out doors and windows. Use your imagination – anything that can be used to create a sense of private space will do.

HIDEOUT SUPPLIES Depending on its size, you may want to install some basic furniture in your shelter – old cable spools make great tables. Rocks or wooden boxes can be chairs. A cooler may also come in handy – it can double as a chair and you can store any provisions in it that you need for a day of adventuring.

WATCHING FOR WILDLIFE Many species will be scared off by the sight of a human being, so making a hideout among the natural vegetation will increase your chances of seeing something. Choose somewhere you know the animal or bird you're waiting to see likes to go, construct your hideout, then climb inside and wait quietly to see what comes along.

TOP TIP

You may need to add some extra camouflage to your hideout if you don't want it to be discovered by anyone else when you're not there or if you want it better disguised when watching for the local wildlife. A few well-placed limbs from a nearby tree or bush will cover up your structure nicely.

SPOTTING WILDLIFE

At first glance the woodland landscape might seem deserted and lifeless. But watch carefully and you'll find many animals going about their business. All you need to know is where to look. Some animals, especially squirrels, venture out at regular intervals to look for something to eat. Throughout the year they bury stores of acorns and nuts that they can depend on during winter when food is scarce.

SKILL LEVEL	★
TIME NEEDED	1 hour

1 Identify a place to look for wildlife. Nature reserves are best, but plenty of animals can be seen even in your own back garden.

2 Find a quiet, comfortable place to watch from – like a window overlooking a garden, or a sheltered spot outdoors near a natural feature that attracts wildlife, such as a lake or woods.

3 Sit still and watch carefully. If you have binoculars, use them to scan the branches of trees – you'll often find birds hopping around. Look carefully near thickets too, as shy animals like foxes often forage beside these sheltered areas.

4 Record what you see on a notepad. If you don't recognize some of the wildlife you encounter, describe its features and behaviour instead: How big is it? What is its shape and colour? Does it hop, fly or crawl? Is it fast or slow moving? These details will help you identify it in a book later.

5 Before you leave, note down the location, time and weather conditions of your visit. That way, if you return to the same spot throughout the year, you can build up a detailed record of how the passing seasons influence wildlife.

YOU WILL NEED

A pair of binoculars (optional, but helpful)

A notepad and pen

INSECT HUNTING

Finding insects isn't hard — there are over 1 million species in the world, from beetles, bees and ants to grasshoppers, butterflies and praying mantises.

SKILL LEVEL	★
TIME NEEDED	1 hour

1 Start by looking under rocks, in soil and in damp, shady areas.

2 Once you find an insect you like, gently pick it up (using the card if you don't want to touch it), drop it in the jar and put the lid on.

3 Sketch the insect and take notes. Compare your notes later with an encyclopaedia or Internet guide to find out more. Then let the insect go – it needs to be in the great outdoors to survive.

YOU WILL NEED

A piece of thin card

A glass jar with a lid

A magnifying glass

A pencil and notebook

REMEMBER!

Don't forget that some insects, like ants, wasps and bees, can give nasty bites or stings.

BIRDWATCHING

Birds are fascinating creatures: from hummingbirds to eagles, they come in every colour of the rainbow and are found on every continent. Birdwatching can be a challenge, both because they're hard to get close to and because they're often well camouflaged. Here are a few tips on how to spot and identify them.

SKILL LEVEL	★★
TIME NEEDED	1–2 hours

1 Get your equipment and head somewhere near water, or a food source like trees with fruit or berries, where birds naturally congregate.

2 Either set up a hideout (see page 26) or find somewhere sheltered to wait quietly.

3 When you spot an interesting bird, train the binoculars on it. Make notes about its size, the shape of its beak, any markings around the head and chest and the shape of its tail feathers.

4 Like all animals, different birds are found in different regions. Use your guide to identify what you've seen from your notes.

YOU WILL NEED

A pair of good binoculars

A pad and pencil

A guide to birds in your region

BUILDING A TREEHOUSE

Building a treehouse is always a great adventure. Once you've finished, it'll make a pefect lookout, fort or base camp. Fit it out with pulleys, climbing ropes and telescopes and you can spend hours exploring without even moving.

SKILL LEVEL	★★★
TIME NEEDED	1 day

1 Start by cutting 45-centimetre (18-inch)-long pieces from your length of wood to make a basic ladder up the trunk of the tree. Pick the exact spot you want to build in and work out how many rungs you'll need on your ladder to climb up to it.

2 Once the pieces have been cut, use at least two nails set side-by-side in each piece to nail the rungs to the tree. Space them about 60 centimetres (2 feet) apart, leading up the trunk to the base of the branches where the platform of the treehouse will be secured.

3 How you access the platform will depend on the shape of your tree. Most of the time, the ladder will come up right under the best branches for building on. That's fine. You'll just have to cut a hole in your floor to climb through. If you keep the piece of wood you cut out, you can use it to make a trap door.

4 Next, haul the sheet of plywood into the tree and position it between the branches where you think it will be most sturdy.

5 Mark the tree limbs with a pencil or nail where the plywood touches them and lower the plywood back down.

6 Cut several more 45-centimetre-long pieces of wood and nail them to the tree at the spots you've marked to act as blocks for your platform.

7 Lift the plywood carefully into place by having two people on the ground pass it up to two people in the tree. Nail the plywood to the blocks.

YOU WILL NEED

A suitable tree (see opposite)

Sturdy length of wood and thick plywood base

A saw (you will need an adult's help to use this)

Galvanized nails

A ladder

A hammer

Rope

8 Next, make railings by nailing up more lengths of plywood between the branches or by tying up pieces of rope to surround your platform.

9 From here you can add a trapdoor using hinges, extra ladder steps leading to higher branches and miniature seats or platforms.

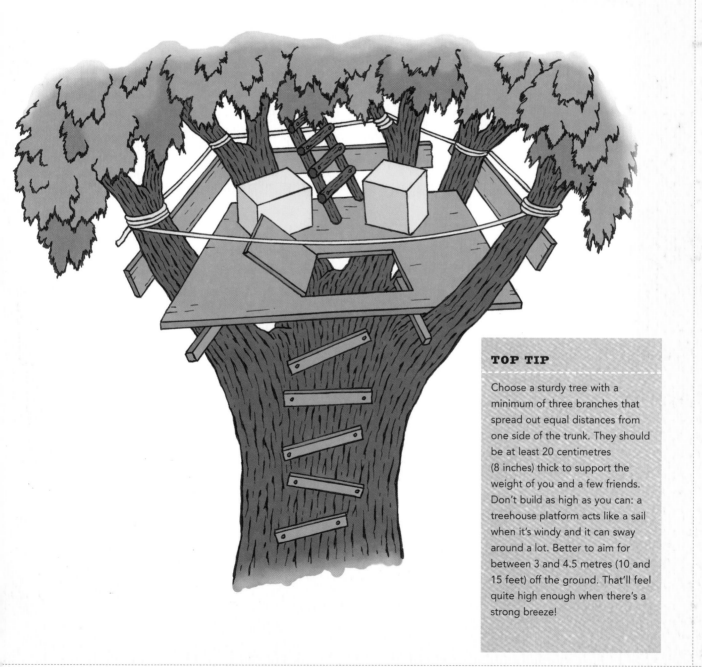

TOP TIP

Choose a sturdy tree with a minimum of three branches that spread out equal distances from one side of the trunk. They should be at least 20 centimetres (8 inches) thick to support the weight of you and a few friends. Don't build as high as you can: a treehouse platform acts like a sail when it's windy and it can sway around a lot. Better to aim for between 3 and 4.5 metres (10 and 15 feet) off the ground. That'll feel quite high enough when there's a strong breeze!

LIGHTING A FIRE WITHOUT MATCHES

Matches were invented in England in 1826 by John Walker. Before that, anyone who wanted to start a fire had to do so either by striking sparks from flint or rubbing two sticks together. The Native Americans devised a technique called 'the bow and drill' in which they used a bow, similar to the bows they used with arrows only much smaller, and a long piece of wood to 'drill' into another piece of wood called the hearth. The friction between the drill and hearth creates enough heat to ignite fur, dried grass and leaves and other tinder. It's not easy, but it will work as long as you're willing to find the right materials and put some energy into the drilling. This technique works best when the drill and the hearth are dry and made of the same type of wood.

SKILL LEVEL	★★
TIME NEEDED	30 minutes

YOU WILL NEED

A teepee of tinder and kindling

A knife

A straight stick of hardwood for the drill

A flat piece of dry hardwood for the hearth

A hand-sized piece of hardwood to use as the socket (this is what you'll hold to press down on the drill when you're turning it)

A cord, shoelace or any other length of tough string

A 30-cm (1 ft)-long stick of flexible wood for the bow

A strong piece of bark

Tinder

1 Before starting, make sure you're positioned close to your teepee of tinder and kindling. Once you get an ember, you'll need to transfer it quickly.

2 Start making your bow and drill by whittling one end of the drill into a point. Round off the other end.

3 Cut a small hole halfway along the hearth about 2.5 centimetres (1 inch) from an edge. The hole should be big enough to allow the rounded end of the drill to fit inside it.

REMEMBER

Always make sure there is an adult present to supervise any activity involving building or lighting a fire.

4 Next, cut a triangular notch in the hearth from the hole to the nearest edge. This will serve as a channel for ashes and embers to spill out onto your tinder.

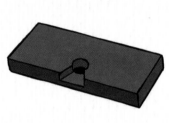

5 You're going to use the socket to press down firmly on the drill. To stop it from slipping, cut a small hole in the socket so that the rounded end of the drill will fit there snugly.

6 Tie the cord or shoelace to the bow. It's helpful to find a bow stick that's already bent, but a freshly cut stick should bend as you tie on the cord.

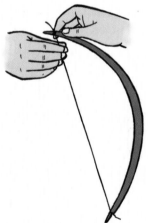

7 Place the hearth on the ground so that the notched side is in contact with a small but strong piece of bark (this is where you will collect the embers).

8 Place the pointed end of the drill in the hole on the hearth. Loop the bow cord over the drill and turn the bow over so that the cord wraps once round the drill. Push down firmly on top of the drill with the socket.

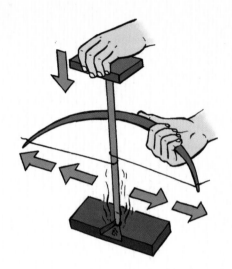

9 Make sawing motions with the bow to work the drill back and forth in a not-too-fast, not-too-slow, steady rhythm. Make sure the drill stays in contact with the hearth. This gets tiring, so you may want a friend to take a turn.

10 Eventually the friction will cause smoke to form and dark brown smoking powder should start rolling down the notch and onto the bark. When smoke appears, increase speed and pressure on the drill.

11 Once the notch is filled with smoking powder and the powder is smoking on its own, gently move the hearth away from the bark and smoking powder. Place the smoking powder onto a small but tight ball of tinder and blow on it until it turns into a glowing red ember. The tinder should also begin to catch fire.

12 Quickly take the smouldering ball of tinder to the teepee of tinder and kindling and place it gently on the tinder platform. Blow on it more if need be until the kindling catches.

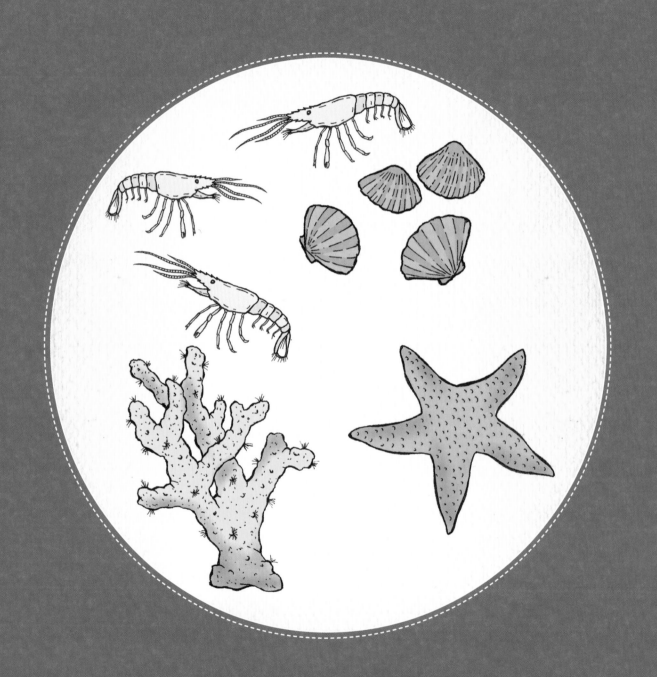

2

WATER ESCAPADES

Whether you're heading to a sandy beach, discovering the magic of rock pools or exploring the hidey-holes of the creek, the water world is a splash of excitement and adventure. With an array of activities for having fun both in the water and beside it, you can get the whole family involved, entertained and maybe a little bit damp.

EXPLORING ROCK POOLS

If you're lucky enough to find rock pools along your beach, then prepare to enter a fascinating world! They're great places to find animals and plants that are completely different from anything you'll see on land. As you investigate the pools, you can imagine you're the first person on a strange and mysterious planet, full of weird and wonderful creatures.

SKILL LEVEL	★
TIME NEEDED	1 hour

YOU WILL NEED

A plastic pail

A shovel

A container with a flat, clear bottom

Sandals

First, get your equipment ready. Take a plastic pail, a shovel for lifting out shells and turning over rocks and a plastic container with a flat, clear bottom. You should also wear sandals. Not only will this give you extra grip on the slippery surfaces, but it'll also stop any little critters from nipping at your feet! To get a great view of the life in the pools, submerge your clear-bottomed container in the water and simply look through it. Look out for crabs of all sorts hiding under rocks, and tiny fish and shrimp darting around in the water. Carefully turn over rocks to see what is hiding underneath, and don't forget to investigate the strange and colourful plants.

ANEMONES Sea anemones are some of the most colourful creatures you're likely to find in a rock pool. Like barnacles, they can close up when threatened, at which point they look like brown slimy nodules on the rocks. But when they open out, they reveal hundreds of colourful tentacles that wave in the water. They may look pretty, but the tentacles have poison barbs, which sting small fish and other animals so that they can be drawn into the central body and eaten.

CRABS Crabs are 10-legged crustaceans easily recognizable by their pincers. They are found all over the world and vary from less than an inch across the shell to almost 38 centimetres (15 inches) for deep-sea varieties! They eat algae and small sea creatures, like tiny shrimps and worms. You may also find hermit crabs, which make their homes in the discarded shells of sea snails and other animals.

REMEMBER!

There are always dangers when exploring so beware! Rock pools are submerged at high tide – it's the fresh water coming in with the tide that keeps them full of life. Be careful of wet, slippery surfaces, and make sure you can easily get to dry land when the tide comes in!

If you lift a rock, you should always put it back where you found it, so the creatures' homes aren't disturbed. You should never remove living creatures from their habitat – if you do want to show others what you've found, call them over and let them see for themselves. You can collect empty shells and colourful stones that you find. These can be great decorations for your sandcastles and sculptures.

HOW TIDES WORK

The great thing about exploring rock pools is that they are constantly refreshed by the high tides. That means what you find one day will be gone and replaced with other wildlife the next. But why does the water level change in the ocean? It's all down to the moon – the gravitational force of the moon pulls the ocean towards it, creating a bulge of water when the moon is overhead. Interestingly, a bulge is created on the opposite side of the Earth too. Scientists believe this is because the Earth itself is pulled slightly towards the moon and away from the water on its opposite side! Because the moon makes a full rotation around the Earth every 24 hours and 50 minutes, there will be a high tide somewhere in the world every 12 hours and 25 minutes or so.

BARNACLES

Barnacles are small shellfish that grow on almost any underwater surface. When out of the water, they seal themselves up to look like small, white stars on the rocks. When they're covered by water again, their tops open out to reveal feathery fronds (actually the animal's legs) that capture plankton from the water for food. The legs will disappear quickly back into the shell if the water around them is disturbed, so you have to be very patient and careful if you want to see them feeding.

SHRIMP Shrimp are crustaceans, like crabs, but have long, thin bodies instead of short, round ones. Their legs are also long and thin and they swim by waving their legs and tails, rather than scuttling around like crabs. There are thousands of different species visible all over the world. Larger shrimp can be cooked and eaten, but the small ones are more fun to observe.

EXPLORING SEA CAVES

If you find a beach surrounded by rocky limestone or chalky cliffs or rock piles, there's a good chance you can find a sea cave. And if you can find a sea cave, you're in for an adventure.

SKILL LEVEL	★
TIME NEEDED	1½–2 hours

Sea caves are formed by the constant push and pull of the ocean waves. The rock has literally been eroded by the water over hundreds and thousands of years. Limestone and chalk are softer than most rocks so the likelihood of sea caves will be greater in places with this kind of geography, but the eroding power of water knows no boundaries. Sea caves can be found anywhere and they take on all kinds of shapes both above and below the waterline.

GETTING IN Exploring sea caves can be done in several different ways from snorkelling or kayaking into them during high tide to hiking through them at low tide. Sometimes you can discover caves that are only accessible underwater. You swim down and come up into a magical air-filled cavern lit by blow holes on the ceiling of the cave. You can find out where these are by talking to the locals.

EXPLORING However you gain access to a cave, what you'll find inside verges on the otherworldly. Often there's white calcite glowing on the walls or sand deposits left by the high tide. Algae can line other parts of the cave. Stalactites and stalagmites form on ceilings and floors. And if it's rock-pool discoveries you're after, you'll find life aplenty in a sea cave – and often it will be life you won't find in rock pools out in the bright sunlight, such as white barnacles and plant growth.

SAFETY Going into a cave requires a lot of care. Wet rocks can be slippery and you have to pay special attention to the tides if you enter a cave at low tide. Wear waterproof shoes and consider taking a waterproof flashlight. If you swim in a cave, always pay close attention to tide swells which can push against the rock. Remember that you should never enter a cave alone.

DID YOU KNOW?

One of the world's biggest sea caves is found on Santa Cruz Island off the coast of California. It's called Painted Cave and is 402 metres (1,318 feet) long. The entrance to the cave is about 40 metres (130 feet) high.

ANGLING

Knowing where and how to fish is the next step on this adventure. With a homemade rod and simple bait, you're going to be limited to just dropping your line in the water. Even so, you can take a strategic approach to landing some swimmers. Here are a few pointers:

1 Look for stumps, large rocks and vegetation – these are good places to drop your line. Fish are hunters too, so they're going to be hiding in these nooks and crannies to surprise their prey.

2 When fishing in the morning, especially in cooler weather, fish near the water's surface by tying your float closer to the hook.

3 In hotter weather, or later in the day, fish in deeper waters and try to get your line down as far as possible by tying your float closer to the rod.

4 Move the bait slowly through the water, as though it's alive and swimming. Fish prefer live prey.

5 When you see your float dip below the surface, that means you've got a bite! Pull up on the rod so the hook catches, and little by little pull your prey to shore. Don't pull so hard that the line breaks, or all your hard work will be for nothing.

SKILL LEVEL	★
TIME NEEDED	1 hour

YOU WILL NEED

A hook (or equivalent)

A worm, insect or other bait

LURES

If you can't find a worm, the grasshoppers keep eluding capture and you've eaten all the other potential bait, use a lure. Fish will often bite something that just looks like their normal food. Simply attach a lure to your hook right above its end, in the hope that the fish will swallow the whole thing.

Potential lures

• Feather
• Bottle cap
• Button
• Aluminium foil

FISHING

Because it's loaded with protein and vitamins, fish is an ideal food when out on a big adventure. But even if you don't plan to eat what you catch, fishing is a fun activity for a lazy afternoon by the water. You can land one just to observe the underwater creature and then return it to its watery life.

SKILL LEVEL	★
TIME NEEDED	1 hour

HOW TO MAKE A FISHING ROD

It's not the only way to catch a fish, but a fishing rod is the easiest. With a few supplies and a long, straight stick, you can make a good one in less than an hour.

1 First, you need to find the right kind of stick. Bamboo works well because it can bend just enough without breaking if you catch a big one. Otherwise, a trimmed tree branch will do fine.

2 Cut a piece of line about the same length as your pole. Fishing line is strong and light, but very thin so fish can't see it in the water.

3 Tie the fishing line around the narrow end of your stick (the thicker end will be your handle).

4 Tie the line around your float about 30 centimetres (1 foot) from the end of the stick. Tie the hook to the very end of your line and you're ready for some bait.

YOU WILL NEED

A 3-m (10 ft)-long stick or bamboo cane

A fishing line

A fishing hook and float (old corks make good floats)

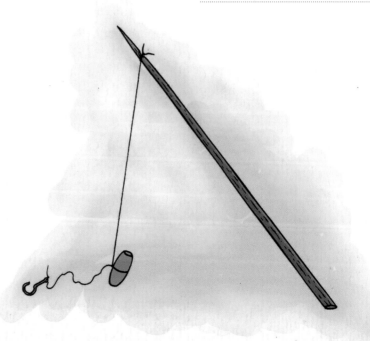

HOW TO BAIT A HOOK

You don't have to use professional hooks to catch a fish. Bent nails, pins, pieces of wire and even sharp thorns can work too.

SKILL LEVEL	★
TIME NEEDED	5 minutes

1 To hook a worm, thread the hook through the head and run the hook through the body until the end is in the worm's tail.

2 If your worms aren't big enough to thread over the hook in this manner, you can use several worms – just be sure to fully cover the hook.

3 For insects, use a segment of thin metal wire and use it to wrap the bait around the hook. Do not damage the insect's body.

4 To bait small live fish or minnows, slide the hook in through the lower and upper lip or along the back (but avoid the spine). These techniques allow the fish to stay alive and swim as it normally would, which is appealing for the larger fish you're trying to catch.

YOU WILL NEED

A hook (or equivalent)

A worm, insect or other bait

CHOOSING BAIT

If you can find a worm, use that to bait your hook. Fish love worms. If you can't find one, there are lots of other things a fish will gladly bite. Pay attention to your surroundings. More often than not, fish dine on the insects and vegetation that is locally available. Your chances of catching a fish will be better if you tempt them with something familiar.

Potential bait:
• Worm
• Grasshopper
• Fly
• Berry
• Bit of bread
• Cheese

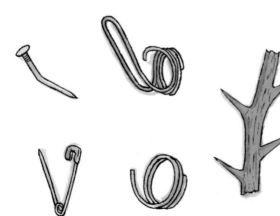

WAVE JUMPING

You can still have fun in the waves even if you don't fancy surfing or bodysurfing: from bobbing up and over them, to diving straight into them and harmlessly out the other side as the tops break over and past you. It's even fun trying to jump over a wave and having the curling lip hit you in the legs and flip your body over. If you're going to try that, timing is everything.

SKILL LEVEL	★
TIME NEEDED	15 minutes

Most waves occur because of distant winds that push the surface of the ocean. They can grow the further they travel and they don't stop until they break on the beach. Waves that have travelled a long way, with strong and consistent winds out at sea, can be really huge and these are good for surfing.

You don't really want to swim in waves over, say, 1.5 metres (5 feet) high. If these break on top of you they can push you down to the seabed and drag you along helplessly. Best to stick to the smaller ones and only swim where there's a sandy bottom instead of a coral bottom, which can tear you up.

For smaller waves you might get a kick out of letting one crash on top of you, but even then you'll feel the awesome power of all that water and energy pushing you around. If the waves are dauntingly big, best to treat a day of swimming with the waves as a game of keep away – you trying to keep away from the break of the white water.

DID YOU KNOW?

The tallest wave ever recorded was an astonishing 30 metres (100 feet) in height – that's the equivalent of seven double-decker buses, or a nine storey building! Generated by an earthquake deep beneath the sea floor, this colossal wave crashed ashore in Alaska in 1958. Luckily, not much damage was done as there weren't any towns nearby.

BEACH COMBING

The beach doesn't just provide a site for fun activities, it's also a treasure trove of unexpected gems and trinkets, such as sea glass, pebbles, shells and even fossils that have been washed up on the shore. Armed with a rake or trowel and a small bag, you can spend hours of adventure playing the amateur archaeologist, hunting for flotsam and jetsam. Maybe you'll find a few tokens to take back home or to hang around your neck for good luck.

SKILL LEVEL	★
TIME NEEDED	30 minutes–1 hour

YOU WILL NEED

A local tide chart

A small rake or trowel

A bag

1 Check local tide charts. The best time to go is during low tide, or after a big storm when the winds will have tossed up lots of debris.

2 To increase your chances of finding good stuff, check peninsular sandbars (which will be visible when the tide is out).

3 Try an area of the beach that isn't too crowded. Densely pebbled sections are also harder to comb.

4 Use a small rake or trowel to dig out possible shells and other treasures when you see the tips of them sticking up.

5 Use a bag to collect interesting objects you might find washed up on the shore, such as bottle tops and sea glass. Examine natural treasures carefully before placing them back where you found them.

BUILDING A SANDCASTLE

Nothing defines a day at the beach like building a sandcastle. Building with sand is fun, relaxing, creative and attention-grabbing. It's also something you can do on your own or you can get the whole family to pitch in and help.

SKILL LEVEL	★
TIME NEEDED	1 hour

You can use the simplest tools like a plastic pail and a shovel, or you can get serious and bring in a raft of clay-sculpting tools like trowels, pointed sticks, chisels and brushes. Plan in advance and bring plastic pails and containers of varying sizes – large, bin-sized ones for the base and varying smaller containers to build up (individual yoghurt containers make for good tops). Last but not least, collect some shells to decorate the rims of towers and walls.

YOU WILL NEED

A variety of different-sized containers

A small shovel

Sand

Detail tools

Collected items (seaweed, shells)

CHOOSING YOUR SITE

The right type of sand is the key to any sandcastle. It has to be wet but not so wet that it falls apart. Here's a good test: find the high-tide line where the darker, wet sand begins to blend into the dry sand that blows easily. Then pick up a fistful of wet sand, compress it into a ball and roll it along the beach. If it remains intact, it's good for building. If it falls apart, it's not wet enough.

Next, find a good flat location where you can build – a good spot is usually a bit further up the beach from the wet sand you need to build with. Not only will the land be flatter further from the tide but you'll be safe from rogue waves or high tide. If you decide to build on a spot well beyond the tide line, you'll need to carry a supply of wet sand up to your building site, so get the shovels and pails, and start digging and hauling! Just pile the wet sand up when you get to your site. Or fill up a pail with water and mix it with the dry sand for more building materials.

Before you start building, pour several pails of water on the area where you plan to erect your castle. Then pack down the area and smooth it to make a firm, flat platform foundation.

All sandcastles start with a central structure or tower. Then you can build out from that by connecting walls to outer turrets and a circular wall. Use the following steps to get started.

TOP TIPS

Carve sand in a gentle shaving method rather than trying to remove large chunks.

Wear sunscreen and a hat! Big sandcastles can take a while to build and hours under the hot sun can give you a bad sunburn.

Keep a spray bottle filled with water handy, so that you can keep the surface sand wet. This helps prevent the sand from crumbling during the building process.

1 Fill your largest container with sand and compress it down as much as possible to remove any air spaces or pockets of dry sand.

2 Turn the container upside down on the centre of your foundation and tap the sides and top with your hands to loosen the sand from the insides of the container. Lift the container up and off the moulded sand structure. This is your first storey. Don't worry if some sand falls away. This can be fixed later.

3 Continue packing sand in smaller containers and stacking them up to make the central tower as tall as you like.

4 Once you get it to the height you want, get out the detail tools (plastic cutlery work just as well as anything) and start carving in windows, turrets, stairs, arrow slits, ramps and whatever else your imagination comes up with. Start at the top and work your way down.

5 After the central tower is built, mould walls with your hands. They should be wide at the bottom and thinner as they go up. Carve arched doorways into walls. Outer towers can be built in the same way the central tower was.

6 Once you're happy with the structure, decorate it with seaweed, shells, beach glass and other found objects.

BEACH ART

Now that you've combed and dug and uncovered the treasures of things that wash up on the beach, what can you do with them? Make stuff, of course. All the shells, driftwood and even sand you find after a morning of combing the shore can be transformed into beach art for your room or a gift for a friend or relative.

SKILL LEVEL	★
TIME NEEDED	1½–2 hours

DRIFTWOOD SHIP SCULPTURE

Use pieces of driftwood to make a ship. This can be as big or as small as you want, but if it gets too big, you might need screws, nails or other fasteners. Best to go small.

YOU WILL NEED

Driftwood

Paints

1 flat, rectangular piece of wood

Wood glue

1 Remove any sand from the driftwood.

2 Paint an ocean scene – waves, seagulls, sun, clouds – on the flat piece of wood.

3 Glue a hull-shaped piece of wood to the front of the flat piece of wood.

4 Next glue on a smoke stack, maidenhead, poop deck and any other extras you can imagine.

5 Paint portholes, an anchor and other colours on the ship and give her a name.

6 Let it dry for at least an hour before taking it home.

SCALLOPED SEASHELL

1 Rinse the salt and sand off of the shells in fresh water and set them out to dry.

2 Paint pictures of seagulls, waves, your dog and anything else you can think of on the inside of each shell. Acrylics work best when you let one colour dry before adding another.

3 When your art is finished – you'll know when – leave them to dry.

YOU WILL NEED

Seashells (chalkier, white shells work best)

Fresh water

Paints (acrylic works best)

Small paintbrush

MAKING A SAND BOTTLE

Here's another fun beach art project involving perhaps the most available material at the beach other than water – sand. It's a great way to create a beautiful souvenir to remind you of a fun day out at the beach. Plus, it's a good way to recycle soda bottles, empty jars and any other glass containers you might find floating or laying around.

1 Cover your piece of wood with the paper and cover the paper with sand. Remove any pebbles or other detritus from the sand.

2 Roll a piece of coloured chalk across the sand until the sand has completely changed to that colour. This should take about five minutes depending on how much sand you have. Don't worry if some of the sand falls off, but try to keep most of it on your work surface.

3 When the sand is the colour you want it, pour it into the bottle using the paper it's on as a funnel.

4 Repeat these steps until you have several colours of sand layered in your bottle and the sand goes all the way to the top.

5 Put the bottle cap on the bottle as tightly as possible.

YOU WILL NEED

A large, flat piece of wood

Paper (newspaper works fine)

Sand

Various colours of chalk

Clear glass bottle or jar with lid

A bottle cap

SKIMMING STONES

By throwing a flat stone into the water in a certain way, it's possible to make it bounce over the surface, whether it's a pond, river or lake. The key to skimming stones is the stone itself. The ideal skimming stone is a flat, oblong-shaped one with round edges. Perfectly round ones are good, but oblong ones give you a place to put your index finger to ensure you get the right spin.

SKILL LEVEL	★
TIME NEEDED	5 minutes

YOU WILL NEED

Water

Flat, oblong-shaped stone with round edges

REMEMBER!

Never skim stones in an area where there are swimmers. Skimmed stones can sometimes move erratically, and nobody likes a stone in the head.

1 Position the stone in your hand so that your thumb is on top of it, your index finger is wrapped around the front edge and your middle and ring fingers are stabilizing it underneath.

2 Stand sideways to the water and pull your arm back, keeping the flat side of the stone parallel to the water.

3 Fling the stone with a side-arm motion. Bend your knees so you get low to the ground. You want the stone to hit the water at as low an angle as possible. Let the stone spin out of your hand and off the end of your index finger so that it spins horizontally, like a Frisbee landing on the water.

4 The harder your first throw is, the more the stone will 'take off' after the first skip. This can be fun, but it can also limit any further skims. Practise to get the speed of throw just right so your stone skips several times.

DIGGING FOR TREASURE

Pirates and the beach go together like seagulls and tuna-fish sandwiches, so why not create your own Treasure Island complete with buried treasure. Unless you're fortunate enough to run across a real map in a nearby sea cave, you'll have to create your own 'X Marks the Spot' and the treasure under it. Or get an adult to set you up.

SKILL LEVEL	★
TIME NEEDED	1 hour

YOU WILL NEED

Rocks

Gold and silver paint

A shoebox

A shovel

Pen and paper

1 Gather some rocks that are nugget-shaped, and paint them gold and silver. This is the actual treasure. Put them in a shoebox. This is the treasure chest.

2 Find a location far from the crowds and, using your shovel, dig a hole about 90-cm (3 feet) deep to bury the 'treasure chest'. After you've filled the hole, mark the spot with an X made of stones, palm fronds or sticks. (To add a challenge to the game, get an adult to bury the treasure so you have to find it first.)

3 Now make your treasure map. After you've marked the spot of the treasure, mark it down on a piece of paper and draw the basic landmark shapes around it – a tree, a lifeguard stand, the ocean.

4 Then count your steps to the nearest landmark and write down how many steps it took to get there. At the same time, draw a dotted line from the landmark to the 'X'.

5 Make your way back to your spot on the beach, counting steps and drawing dotted lines as you go until you have an accurate locator to the treasure.

6 Find the treasure and dig it up!

> **TOP TIP**
>
> Once you have the master map done, you can create alternative maps by leaving clues to the location for prospective treasure hunters instead of giving them the map outright.

3

NATURE CRAFTING

There is a world of adventure to be had in your own back garden or the local park. From making sundials and painting a clay pot to creating a terrarium and building a leaf press, you'll find all sorts of fun projects to keep you and your friends entertained all day long.

CREATING A TERRARIUM

Terrariums are enclosed glass containers filled with soil and plants. Because they're sealed up, water inside condenses on the sides and top of the glass and runs back down into the soil – automatic rain! You hardly ever have to water a terrarium, but you do get to watch the plants grow from seeds to baby plants in a couple of weeks.

SKILL LEVEL	★
TIME NEEDED	1 hour

1 Line the bottom of the jar with peat moss and scatter a layer of gravel over the top.

2 On top of the gravel, put down a layer of potting mix for your plants to grow in. The moss-gravel-soil layers should be at least 7.5 centimetres (3 inches) thick.

3 Plant a few seedlings or plants in the jar – you don't want it to be too crowded. Use long tweezers or tongs to make small holes and to lower plants into the jar. Cover their roots and tamp soil loosely around them. If you're sowing seeds, spread soil lightly over the top.

4 Water the plants lightly – about 125 millilitres (4 fl oz) of water should be enough. If your plants get too wet, the soil will turn to marsh and nothing will grow except mould.

5 Use a screwdriver or other sharp device to poke three or four small holes in the jar lid. Terrariums need ventilation so mould doesn't grow inside. Screw the lid onto the jar.

6 Place the terrarium in a well-lit place near a window, but not in direct sunlight because that can burn the plants inside.

7 Watch your plants grow! If you want to add more life, find a few insects in your garden that eat plants and settle them in. Be careful not to have too many, though, or they'll eat faster than your plants can grow.

8 Every few months, scrape off the top layer of potting soil and replace it with fresh stuff to keep your plants nourished.

YOU WILL NEED

A large glass jar with a wide opening and a metal lid

Clumps or sheets of peat moss

Gravel

Potting mix

Small plants that like humid environments, like spider ferns

Long tweezers or tongs that can fit inside the jar opening

A screwdriver

BUILDING A SUNDIAL

Sundials are the world's oldest clocks — they work on the principle that the sun is always in the same direction at noon: directly south in the Northern Hemisphere, and directly north in the Southern Hemisphere. With your own sundial, you can tell time using the sun and the shadows it creates.

SKILL LEVEL	★
TIME NEEDED	6 hours

1 Turn the shoebox on its end. Draw a circle in the middle of one end.

2 Using a screwdriver, poke a hole in the middle of the circle. Then poke a hole in the bottom of the shoebox below the first hole, but a little further back.

3 Push your stick through the first hole and angle it back towards the end of the shoebox. Push the tip of the stick through the second hole you made and tape it in place. Your stick should now poke up at an angle out of the circle on the top of the box.

4 Take your sundial outside and place it on a flat surface.

5 Use a compass to find north, and point the stick in that direction if you're in the Northern Hemisphere, or south if you're in the Southern Hemisphere. The stick should throw a good, clear shadow across the circle you drew.

6 At exactly 9 a.m., draw a line marking the position of the shadow of the stick on the circle you drew in step 1. Mark it with a straight line and label it 9 a.m..

7 Each hour after that, revisit your sundial and mark the new location of the shadow up until 3 p.m. Your sundial is now ready to tell the time. If you want your sundial to work earlier or later during the day, you have to keep on marking the shadow on the hour.

8 Any time you want to use the sundial, take it outside and use your compass to point the stick in the right direction, as you did in step 5. Then see where the shadow falls across the lines you drew.

YOU WILL NEED

A shoebox

A black marker

A screwdriver

A straight stick – bamboo works well

Masking tape

A compass

A consistently sunny day

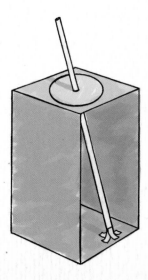

MAKING A PLANT POT

Pottery is one of the oldest human technologies and art forms, and we're still making it today. Here's a chance to try your hand at this craft and make your own little plant pot. The type used by professional potters needs to be fired (baked) at very high temperatures, but you can buy hobby clay from craft stores that will either dry by itself or can be baked in a home oven. This project can get messy, so put on an apron or overall to cover your clothes, and make sure you have a hard, flat surface to work on — one that won't stain.

SKILL LEVEL	★★★
TIME NEEDED	1–2 hours

YOU WILL NEED

Air-dried or home-oven-fired clay

An apron or old shirt (to protect your clothes)

String

Poster paints

Decorations, e.g. fake gems, baubles, glitter, etc. (optional)

1 Warm the clay by kneading it with your hands. If you keep folding it over on top of itself, you will create air bubbles (which you want to avoid) so after kneading, throw the ball back and forth quite roughly between your hands or throw it onto a hard surface (like a worktop) several times.

2 Once the clay is soft and pliable, roll it into a long 'worm' that's about 12 millimetres (½ inch) in diameter and about 30–60 centimetres (12–24 inches) long. Keep the width of the worm as consistent as possible all the way down to avoid bulges in your pot.

3 Take one end of the 'worm' and start to coil it into a tight circle. Continue to coil it around itself, making sure the coils are pressed together, until you've created a circular base for your pot. (You can mould it into a smooth base if you prefer by scraping a straight edge across the surface.) Cut the 'worm' where the coil finishes and secure the end by moulding it onto the coil.

4 Now you can start the sides of the pot. Take the end of your clay 'worm' and coil it around the outside of the base. Press it down firmly and then, on the inside of your pot (while supporting the outside wall with the other hand so it doesn't bow out), smooth down with your fingertips to seal the gap between the bottom and the coil.

5 As you reach the end of the first coil, allow the worm to overlap and continue building the wall, smoothing down each time.

6 Once you've reached the desired height (or the end of your worm), level out the top row by flattening it down slightly and trimming down the end.

7 Make sure the inside is completely smoothed out – wetting your fingers makes this easier.

8 If you are having trouble removing your pot from the work surface, take a piece of string and wrap it around a couple of fingers on both hands (rather like dental floss) and, pulling the string tight, 'saw' it back and forth, pulling it towards you underneath the pot.

9 If you're using home-oven clay, then follow the instructions that came with it to bake it solid. This clay is best baked on an oven-safe glass surface. For air-dry clay, just leave the pot out overnight until it hardens.

10 Once your clay is fully dry, you can paint the pot. Put on two coats, and glue on any other decorations you fancy.

BUILDING A LEAF PRESS

Everything in nature happens for a reason and the colours
of leaves are no different. If you want to preserve some
colourful leaves so they don't go brown, you can build a press.
Here's how:

SKILL LEVEL	★★
TIME NEEDED	1–2 hours

1 Lay one of the boards flat on a table and cover it with three or four layers of tissue paper. Make sure there are no wrinkles or creases in the paper, and it's as smooth as possible.

2 Choose your favourite leaves and lay them on the tissue paper. Leave at least a 1 centimetre (½ inch) gap between neighbouring leaves.

3 Cover the leaves with another three or four layers of tissue paper. Make sure it stays smooth. Put the other board on top.

4 Finally, either screw clamps tightly at each end of the boards, or pile plenty of heavy books or even bricks on top.

5 Leave the whole setup in a cool, dry place and the moisture will be squeezed out of the leaves and drawn into the tissue paper. After a few weeks, you will be left with dried-out, flattened leaves, with the autumn colours preserved.

YOU WILL NEED

Two pieces of plywood at least
15 cm (6 in) wide on each side

Tissue paper

Colourful leaves

Two clamps (or a large pile of heavy
books)

DID YOU KNOW?

Leaves are green because they contain a substance called chlorophyll. A tree spends a lot of energy making more chlorophyll for its leaves so it can continue to grow. During winter, trees will stop making chlorophyll and hibernate to conserve their energy for the spring. When the tree stops replenishing chlorophyll, the green colour goes out of the leaves and other colours start to show through. The yellow-brown, red and purple colours come from chemicals already in the leaf. They are always there – we just can't see them the rest of the time because the green chlorophyll usually covers them up.

LEAF RUBBING

While away a sunny afternoon with some fabulous leaf-rubbing designs. With a little patience and a lot of imagination, you can produce some wonderful nature-themed patterns.

1 Collect a selection of leaves in different shapes and sizes. Place the leaves, vein side up, on a sheet of white paper in any pattern you like, and put the second sheet of white paper on top of your design.

2 Take off any paper wrapping around your crayons. Using the long side of a crayon rather than the tip, rub gently over the sheet. The outline of your leaves will appear and reveal your designs.

3 We tend instinctively to turn to autumnal shades of browns, russets and greens when leaf rubbing but you can actually use any colour, however vibrant, in your design. Go crazy and see what works for you!

YOU WILL NEED

A selection of leaves

2 sheets of plain white paper

A packet of coloured crayons

GROWING A SUNFLOWER

Growing plenty of colourful flowers can instantly transform your garden into your own little summer retreat, and few flowers are as summery as the sunflower. It's also a great place to start for those of you who are looking for a challenge because sunflowers can be a bit tricky to grow.

SKILL LEVEL	★
TIME NEEDED	15 minutes to plant, 2–3 months to grow

1 In spring, after the danger of frost has passed, find a clear flowerbed in a nice, sunny spot and loosen the soil with a trowel. Then plant your seeds 10–15 centimetres (4–6 inches) apart and cover them with 12 millimetres (½ inch) of soil.

2 Water them just enough to keep the soil moist – don't overwater them or they won't grow. Keep watering them as the seeds sprout and your miniature sunflower plants start to develop. Check the soil once or twice a week to make sure that it's not bone-dry. Your plants should soon start to shoot up into tall, straight stems with large, flat leaves.

3 Expect the flowers to develop in the late summer and early autumn. As the flowers start to fade, cut the dead heads off to encourage new flowers to grow in their place.

4 If your variety is an annual (i.e. has a lifespan of just one year), pull the plants out and discard them in the autumn, once they have been exposed to frost. If you chose a perennial variety (i.e. one that blooms each year), then just cut them down and wait until next year for them to flower again.

5 You can give your sunflower a head start during a cold spring by planting the seed in a little pot on your windowsill and letting it grow into a seedling indoors. Then you can plant the seedling rather than seeds in your garden. Don't forget to water your little pot regularly, or your seedlings won't get started!

YOU WILL NEED

A garden trowel

Sunflower seeds (available from garden centres and supermarkets)

A watering can

GROWING HERBS

Herbs have been used for thousands of years. They have been added to dishes, used as perfumes, remedies and even as currency. These days you're most likely to use them in the kitchen to add flavour to your food, and there are all sorts of different herbs available. Growing your own herbs means you'll always have an abundance of different ones to try.

SKILL LEVEL

TIME NEEDED 20 minutes to plant, 4–6 weeks to grow

1 Make sure all of your chosen containers have good drainage. If you're using plastic pots, you can carefully poke a hole in the bottom with an awl or a screwdriver.

2 Fill the containers three-quarters full with potting mix.

3 When choosing your herbs, think about which ones might smell good. Do you like mint and basil, or maybe rosemary and thyme?

4 Don't forget to check the labels to see how big the plants can grow. Make sure your garden won't get so big it takes over the whole kitchen!

5 Allocate herbs to each pot according to how big the plants grow.

6 Tip the seedlings out of their little pots and plant them in your containers. Surround them with more potting mix, press down a little to make sure they're secure (but not so much that the soil is packed together) and give them some water.

7 Arrange your pots attractively on a windowsill where they will get plenty of sunlight, and watch them grow!

8 Make sure your containers are well watered because the herbs tend to dry out more quickly in pots than if they were planted in the garden.

YOU WILL NEED

Containers of various sizes

Good multipurpose potting mix

Your choice of herb seedlings in pots (available from garden centres)

A trowel

NATURE PHOTOGRAPHY

Years ago, photography was a very skilled hobby, but modern technology means it is now much easier to get good results. Even a basic digital camera can be used to take impressive pictures that you can share with your friends in print or on a computer. Get in the habit of taking a camera with you on walks and trips outside and soon enough you'll spot something striking or beautiful that deserves to have its picture taken.

SKILL LEVEL	★★
TIME NEEDED	1 hour

YOU WILL NEED

A camera

A computer (optional)

1 On a day when the light is strong and clear, go outside with your camera. Look for a special feature that catches the eye, or try taking photos across different seasons to capture the changes in nature.

2 Looking through the viewfinder of the camera, or the digital viewing screen at its rear, carefully frame the feature you are interested in. Get as close to the subject as you can while still keeping all of the features you want inside the shot.

3 If possible, it's better to have the sun shining from behind you when you take the picture. That way, the object you want to photograph will be well lit and your camera will not be 'dazzled' by light shining directly at it from in front.

4 If you are taking a picture of a landscape, make sure the horizon is straight rather than tilted in the viewfinder. Some experts think that positioning the viewfinder so that land fills two thirds of the frame and sky fills the last third (or vice versa) makes for a good picture – try both ways and see if you agree.

5 After you have taken your pictures, it's time to view them. If you have a digital camera, you can look at the images right away on a home computer, provided you have the correct connecting cable. Ask an adult to help if you're not sure. If you also have a printer on hand, you can buy special photographic paper that will allow you to make high-quality prints of your pictures at home.

6 Alternatively, you can take your camera to a professional photography store with printing facilities. Ask the staff to help you choose what kind of prints to have made. This will cost money, so get permission from an adult first.

THE GOLDEN RATIO

The Golden Ratio is a guideline that can be used to draw the human eye into the composition of a photograph, based on the ratio of placement of the different elements in the picture. It is a constant, often expressed as 1.618 (although this is what is known as an irrational number – the digits after the decimal point go on for ever). Although the number was primarily applied in maths, many Renaissance painters and architects used the Golden Ratio in their works, including Leonardo da Vinci, believing it to be aesthetically pleasing.

Imagine you have a straight line divided into two parts, one longer length (*a*) and one shorter length (*b*). The Golden Ratio is when the ratio of *b* to *a* is the same as the ratio of *a* to the whole line. So if *a* is about 1.618 times greater than *b*, you've divided it into the Golden Ratio.

BALLOON GREENHOUSE

Growing plants can be great fun, but is usually just a spring and summer activity. Here is a different way to experiment with growing seeds, and by adding a little science these can grow all year round.

SKILL LEVEL   ★

TIME NEEDED 15 minutes to plant, 2–4 months to grow

1 Inflate your balloon to its full size, to make sure that the balloon is see-through. Then deflate the balloon

2 Insert the funnel in the neck of the balloon and use this to put soil into the balloon so that it is full.

3 Now add the seeds using the funnel. It is best to choose plants that are small when grown, but you can experiment with different types/ sizes of flowers.

4 Reinflate the balloon to its full size, tie the end and mix the seeds into the soil by shaking the balloon.

5 Find a place outside for the balloon where it will get the sun for at least half the day or more.

6 Don't worry about watering as when the balloon cools in the evening it will condensate on the inside and water your seeds during the day – you can just watch them grow!

YOU WILL NEED

White balloons

A funnel

Fine damp soil

Mixed seeds

BUILDING A PARK

Going to the park can be great fun — we all like the rides and challenges a park can have. This crafting activity allows you to build your own imaginary park using a mixture of natural and manmade materials.

SKILL LEVEL ★ ★

TIME NEEDED 30–40 minutes

1 Find a small area on the ground where you can lay out a circle of rope about the size of a hula-hoop. If you do not have an outdoor space, this activity can be done in a shoebox.

2 Think about parks you have visited for inspiration, as well as using your imagination. It can be a water park, theme park or wildlife park – the choice is yours.

3 Starting by using only natural resources, build your miniature dream park. You can use bits of dead wood, moss, leaves, pine cones or even bury a small yoghurt pot filled with water to create a small pond.

4 When you have finished building give your park a name. Think about who will visit, what the opening times will be, whether it is free to enter and any other information you may want to include.

5 You can also try following the same steps to create a mini beast park, using natural materials to attract wildlife into this small area.

YOU WILL NEED

A piece of rope/string/wool about 2.5m (8 ft) long

Shoebox (optional)

Your choice of natural resources

Your choice of manmade resources

MESSAGE IN A BOTTLE

Think of a message in a bottle and it might conjure up visions of desperate castaways trying to get off their deserted islands. But they can be a fun way to pass messages among your friends along rivers and small bodies of water.

SKILL LEVEL	★
TIME NEEDED	30 minutes

1 Write a note. Always write in pencil because it won't fade or smudge in the elements. Be sure to include your name, date and address so the friend who finds it can trace it back to you.

2 Staple or glue a ribbon to a corner of the note. Then roll up your note around the pencil.

3 Holding the other end of the ribbon, drop your note and pencil into the bottle.

4 Secure the ribbon to the bottom of your cork (again with glue or the stapler), and press the cork firmly into the bottle until it's snug.

5 Heat the wax in a pot. Once it has melted, dip the corked end of your bottle in to seal it.

6 When you're ready, toss the bottle into the water, making sure the current is travelling in the direction of your friend downstream. (Otherwise your bottle may not reach its intended recipient and risks polluting the environment.)

YOU WILL NEED

Paper

A pencil

A stapler or glue

A thick glass bottle with a cork

Ribbon

Wax

A pot

DID YOU KNOW?

During the 1500s in England sending a message in a bottle was a royally-sanctioned means of communication. In fact, floating messages were used by the British fleet to Queen Elizabeth I and she employed an official 'Uncorker of Ocean Bottles'. It was a crime for anyone else to open a bottle with a message in it. Later, in the United States, Benjamin Franklin charted ocean currents by dropping bottles into the Gulf Stream and finding out where they went when the bottles were discovered and returned to him from afar through the mail.

MAKING AN ORIGAMI BOAT

Whether you're at a lake, pond or river, having a boat to float on the water is a great summer's activity. If you forgot to bring one along, it's easy to make your own out of paper.

SKILL LEVEL   ★

TIME NEEDED   10 minutes

The hobby of folding paper, more commonly known as origami, goes back many centuries. Although paper was introduced to Japan from China in the sixth century, folding paper to make models only became popular in the 1600s. The earliest designs were simple but now origami enthusiasts can make the most intricate and beautiful models of flowers, animals and birds – and all without the use of a single pin, dot of glue or a stapler!

YOU WILL NEED

A large, rectangular sheet of coloured paper – the brighter the better!

1 Fold the paper in half widthways and make a crisp crease in the middle.

2 Bring each of the top corners in to meet in the middle, forming a triangular point. Crease the folds so that it lays flat.

3 Fold the bottom edge upward, so that the fold is level with the bottom of the triangle. Then flip it over and fold the other edge up in the same way.

4 Hold the triangle point-down, with your thumbs inside, and pull it open so that the sides come together. Press them flat and you should be left with a diamond shape.

5 At the open end of the diamond, fold each side down to make another triangle. Then pull it open as you did before to make another diamond.

6 Now turn the diamond upside-down and pull the sides away from the middle. With a little careful shaping, you'll end up with a beautiful paper boat with high prow and stern and a triangular mast.

TOP TIP

To ensure you get a neat-looking model, make the folds as crisp as possible by running your fingernail along the edge to flatten the fold, and keep the corners neat by using the tip of your nail or a ballpoint pen to guide the fold to produce a sharp edge.

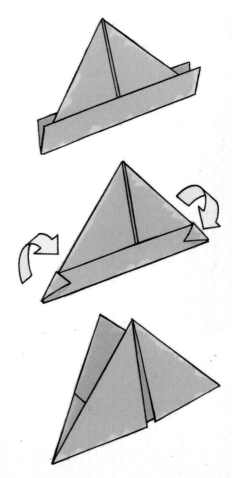

MAKING AND FLYING A KITE

Reach up to the skies with a homemade kite. This can be quite challenging so an adult pair of hands is probably a good idea. Make sure any decoration you add is even so that your kite stays balanced – if you have too much weight on one side, the kite will spin out of control when the wind blows and crash rather than fly.

SKILL LEVEL	★★
TIME NEEDED	45 minutes

1 Cut thin, shallow notches in the ends of both pieces of cane. These notches don't have to be thicker than the blade of a knife.

2 Make a cross by placing the shorter piece of cane over the longer piece. They should intersect about 30 centimetres (1 foot) down on the longer piece.

3 Secure them in place by lashing them with thick twine. Pass the twine around the crossing point in an 'X', and tuck the end under the loops to finish off.

4 Now make a tight frame of twine around the canes, using the notches you made in step 1 as guides. First make a loop in the end of the twine, using a bowline knot. Lodge the knot on one notch (so the loop hangs free the other side) and stretch the string all the way around, passing through each notch until you come back to the loop.

5 Pass the twine through the loop and stretch it back around the frame in the reverse direction. Repeat steps 4 and 5 a few times. This will make the twine frame taut. Be careful not to make it too tight or the canes will warp.

6 Lay the cane and twine frame over your sheet of paper. Trace around the kite frame onto the paper, giving yourself at least 2.5 centimetres (1 inch) of extra paper all around the outline.

7 Cut the shape of the kite out of the paper. Don't forget to make the paper a little larger than the kite. Attach the paper to the face of the cane kite frame by folding the extra width of paper over the twine all the way around, and taping it to the back.

YOU WILL NEED

1 straight, thin piece of cane about 90 cm (3 ft) long

1 straight, thin piece of cane 45 cm (18 in) long

A good, long piece of thick twine

A long kite string

Scissors

A large piece of thick white paper, at least 90 x 30 cm (3 x 1 ft)

Masking tape

Ribbon

8 Create the kite 'harness' by tying a piece of twine at the top and bottom of the long piece of cane, and another piece at the ends of the shorter piece of cane. They should intersect about 15 centimetres (6 inches) above the intersection of the canes. Tie the two pieces of twine together at that point and make a small twine loop in one of the tied ends. This is where you'll attach your kite string when you're ready to fly.

9 Make a kite tail with a 90-centimetre (3-foot) length of twine. Tie 10-centimetre (4-inch) pieces of ribbon to the twine every 15 centimetres (6 inches), or as you like.

10 Tie the kite string to the loop and you're ready to take your kite outside on a windy day and launch!

11 Find a large open area free of trees and electrical lines. Let out a small length of kite string and, holding the string in your hand, run with the kite behind you into the wind until it lifts it. Keep letting out string until the kite reaches a good height.

12 Keep an eye on your kite, in case the wind drops. Run into the wind or pull on the string to give your kite some extra lift.

13 Bring the kite down by slowly winding the kite string around your hand and catch it just before it hits the ground to avoid damaging it.

REMEMBER!

Stay away from electrical lines. If your kite becomes entangled, leave it there. Never fly your kite during a thunderstorm.

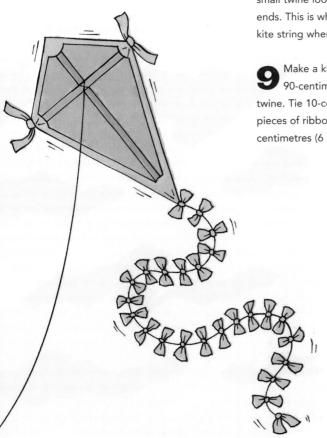

MAKING A BASKET

Basket weaving is one of the oldest known crafts, even pre-dating pottery making, and the skill has been handed down through the generations. If you imagine that practically any container or packaging that is now made from plastic, cardboard, or plywood would once have been made of basketry, it gives you an idea of the importance of basket makers throughout history. Although it's probably a bit too ambitious to attempt to make a traditional willow basket from scratch, you can start with a paper one to get the hang of the principles.

SKILL LEVEL	★★
TIME NEEDED	45 minutes

1 Cut each sheet of paper into long strips about 12 mm (½ inch) wide. Lay out 12 strips of the same colour (red, for example) next to each other in vertical lines, then count out 12 strips of the other colour (we'll say green for this example).

2 Take a green strip and, starting about a third of the way down, horizontally weave it over the first vertical red strip on the right and under the next, repeating this over and under movement until you reach the other side. Pull the strip through so that you have roughly equal ends protruding on each side of the vertical strips.

3 Take the next green strip and weave it horizontally under the red vertical strips starting just below your first green strip.

YOU WILL NEED

2 large sheets of construction paper in different colours (say green and red)

A stapler or craft glue

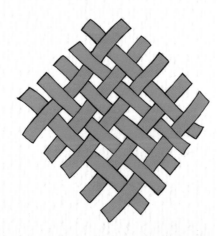

4 Continue weaving the strips until all 24 have been used.

5 Try to keep the weaving as neat and even as possible so that you end up with a reasonably tight checkerboard effect.

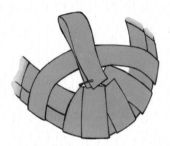

6 You should now have a woven base with green strips extending on two opposite sides and red strips extending on the other two opposite sides.

7 Gather up all of the strips on one side. Bend them upward and collect them into the middle to form a fan shape that is broader at the base, so that all the ends of the strips come together. Staple or glue the ends where they meet.

8 Repeat this step with the strips on the other three sides.

9 Take two more red strips and two more green strips. Put them into pairs (it's up to you whether you mix your colours or keep like with like). Attach one end of one pair of strips to a corner (top of the fan) and cross it over the centre of the basket and attach to the opposite corner.

10 Take the last remaining pair of strips and repeat step 9 using the other two corners of the basket.

11 You can leave your handle plain or you might like to make a paper bow to attach to it as a decoration. These attractive baskets look fabulous filled with brightly wrapped sweets.

4

GADGET-FREE GAMES

Fantastic for groups, outdoor games are fun, active and versatile: you can play them at the park, by the pool or in your own garden. You'll find plenty of tips in this chapter for old favourites, as well as great new ideas. There are silly games like the egg-and-spoon race or more full-on matches like dodgeball. Maybe you want to test your skill at French bowls? Whether you'd prefer something competitive or just want to keep entertained, there are plenty of options to try.

FRENCH BOWLS

The aim of this game is to throw metal balls (boules) as close as possible to a small wooden ball called a jack or *cochonnet* (piglet). Known as *pétanque* in its native France, this game is popular all over the world but never more so than in its homeland where around 17 million French families play it, mostly during their summer vacations. So, mes amis, let's play.

SKILL LEVEL	★
TIME NEEDED	30 minutes–1 hour

1 Mark out a starting line on the ground. The players must stand behind this line when throwing their balls.

2 One of the players throws the jack out at a distance of 6–10 metres (20–30 feet) from the starting point.

3 A teammate then plays the first boule, throwing it so that it ends up as close to the jack as possible.

4 Then the opposing team must throw, trying to get closer to the jack. They keep playing until they succeed. When they do, it is back to the first team to do better, and so forth.

5 When one of the teams runs out of boules, the other team plays their remaining ones.

6 When all boules have been played, that is the end of a 'round' and the winning team scores a point for each boule that is nearer to the jack than the opposing team's nearest boule.

7 The team that wins a round starts the next one, starting from where the jack ended up in the previous round.

8 The game continues until one of the teams has accumulated 13 points.

YOU WILL NEED

Teams of players

A jack (small wooden ball)

A set of boules (metal balls)

Large open space

DODGEBALL

This fast and furious game is so versatile — it can be played indoors or out, you can have as many people in the team as you like and, best of all, you get to throw balls at other people! The rules of dodgeball vary from place to place and school to school, but if you get the hang of these basics, you'll be able to join in and adapt wherever you're invited to play.

SKILL LEVEL	★★
TIME NEEDED	10 minutes–1 hour

1 There is a strip about 0.5 metres (2 feet) wide across the centre of the court called the Dead Zone. You'll need to mark this out if you're creating your own dodgeball court to play on. Three balls are placed in the Dead Zone at the beginning of the game.

2 The two teams (ideally you should have about six people on each team) stand on opposite sides of the Dead Zone.

3 The referee starts the game, which lasts two minutes. Three players from each team run to get the balls. The balls must then be passed to the back line of the court before play starts.

4 The aim is to throw the balls at your opponents (but not at the head), and if they're hit, they are out.

5 If at any time during the game you catch a throw from an opposing player, that person is out and one of your team players comes back in.

6 You win a game when all the opposing team is out, or if you have more players left on court at the end of the two minutes.

YOU WILL NEED

2 teams of 6 players

A space about the size of a badminton or tennis court

3 foam balls

A referee

TOP TIP

Stay inside the court and out of the Dead Zone – if you step over the boundaries, on to the opposing side or into the Dead Zone, you're out. Also watch out for opponents trying to knock the ball from your hands – if they succeed, you're also out.

TUG-OF-WAR

You need plenty of muscle on your side to succeed at tug-of-war, but there's a surprising amount of technique involved too. In fact, brains and brawn are the ideal combination for this game that was originally played by British sailors on their long voyages around the world.

SKILL LEVEL	★
TIME NEEDED	15–30minutes

1 Lay the rope out on the ground.

2 Tie the white handkerchief in the middle of the rope.

3 About 1 metre (3 feet) either side of the handkerchief, mark two lines on the ground intersecting the rope.

4 Each team lines up along the rope, facing each other, and takes hold.

5 Take up the tension and when the referee says 'Go', both teams pull as hard as they can.

6 If the handkerchief crosses the line nea-rest your team, you've won.

YOU WILL NEED

A long rope

A white handkerchief or scarf

2 teams of roughly equal sizes and numbers

BALANCING TUG-OF-WAR

If you have limited numbers and different ages/sizes of player, the following variation can ensure that the biggest doesn't always win.

SKILL LEVEL	★★
TIME NEEDED	15 minutes –½ hour

1 Place the stools about 2–4 metres (6–12 feet) apart.

2 Lay the rope between the stools, leaving any surplus coiled up at both ends.

3 A player stands on each stool and holds the rope. On starter's orders, you can pull or relax the rope, trying to get the other player to lose balance and step off. Brute strength is not always the answer in this variation. If you tug too hard and your opponent loosens his or her grip, the sudden slack may cause you to fall off.

YOU WILL NEED

2 sturdy crates or stools

A long rope

REMEMBER!

This activity is best played on soft ground in case someone takes a tumble from the stool.

CROQUET

Think of croquet and you'll probably picture a group of ladies in white dresses and parasols playing on the lawn on a hot summer's day in the early 1900s. Actually, the game is still popular today, although, admittedly, it tends to be played with a bit more gusto.

SKILL LEVEL	★★
TIME NEEDED	30 minutes

1 First you need to set up the croquet hoops and agree to the order and direction you are going to play each one. You must hit the ball through each hoop in the agreed direction, or it doesn't count.

2 One team plays the blue and black balls and is known as the 'cool' team, and the other team plays the red and yellow balls of the set and is known as the 'hot' team.

3 The team that goes first plays the blue and black balls. They take turns following the colours on the stake; for example, blue first, yellow last.

4 Place your ball 1 metre (3 feet) south of the first hoop and try to hit it through. You earn another turn if you succeed. If not, your turn is over.

5 If your ball goes through and comes to rest touching another player's ball, you get two bonus strokes (this is known as a 'croquet'). You cannot croquet the other team's balls more than once each turn, unless your ball passes through a hoop, but then you still must not croquet the same ball twice in succession.

6 Your ball must pass through the hoops in the agreed order around your course.

7 Once your ball has passed through all of hoops twice (in the right order!), you have to aim for the post. (If you hit the post at any point during the game, you must return your ball to the start.)

YOU WILL NEED

2 teams

A croquet set (comprising 9 hoops, 2 posts or stakes, 4 mallets and 4 balls)

A lawn

8 Take your ball out of play when it hits the final stake.

9 The first team to hit the final stake with both balls is the winner.

THREE-LEGGED RACE

A firm favourite of the parish picnic, the three-legged race is also popular with university students as an annual fundraising event. It's ridiculous, it's clumsy and no one is too young (or too old!) to join in with this laugh-a-minute game. Get everyone tripping over themselves!

SKILL LEVEL	★★
TIME NEEDED	1 hour

1 Use the two ropes to mark a starting line and a finish line. Divide players into pairs. Each player stands next to his partner and puts his arm around his partner's waist.

2 The partners' inside legs should be touching. Tie the partners' inside legs together so each pair has three legs rather than four.

3 The players line up at the starting line. On the signal, players walk or run as fast as they can to the finish line.

4 Sound easy? You'll be surprised how difficult it can be to make two legs work as one! The winners are the pair that crosses the finish line first.

YOU WILL NEED

2 ropes

Scarves or strips of fabric long enough for tying legs together (one for each pair of contestants)

SACK RACE

If you can complete the whole course without falling down, you're a better sack racer than most! But then, falling down is half the fun of this crazy game.

SKILL LEVEL	★
TIME NEEDED	1 hour

1 Using the ropes, lay out a start line and a finish line.

2 Each contestant climbs into a sack, holding the edges of the sack up around their waist.

3 On the starter's whistle, they must hop from the start line to the finish line.

4 If you fall down (and you probably will) just get up and carry on once you've managed to stop laughing!

YOU WILL NEED

Ropes

Some old pillowcases or burlap sacks

EGG-AND-SPOON RACE

This time-honoured playground game requires just the right mix of balancing skills and patience combined with speed and agility. Can you keep the egg on the spoon in the final dash to the line?

SKILL LEVEL	★
TIME NEEDED	1 hour

1 Use the rope to lay out a start line and a goal line. Players line up at the start line, balancing the egg on their spoon (remember: you are not allowed to steady the egg with your thumb).

2 When the whistle blows, the first person to get up to the goal line and back without dropping their egg is the winner. (If you drop it, don't worry, you just have to pick it up and carry on!)

3 Whoever makes it back to the start line first is the winner!

YOU WILL NEED

Dessert spoons

Hard-boiled eggs

2 or more players

Rope

REMEMBER!

Because it is so easy to trip and fall during these races, make sure you set your course on grass or some other soft surface.

LEAPFROG

Believe it or not, there is evidence that the Ancient Egyptians played Leap Frog, which they called Knuzza Iawizza. Seems that a good playground game will always stand the test of time. So why not put a spring in your step and give it a try.

SKILL LEVEL	★
TIME NEEDED	5 minutes

1 Each player stands side by side in a line, spaced out, and, when in position, the players should kneel down and rest their heads on the ground, covered by their hands.

2 Stand at the back of the line, and place your hands on the back of the person at the back of the line. Press down on the person's back and leap over them, spreading your legs apart like a frog.

3 Continue hopping over players until you reach the front of the line, where you then kneel down and cover your head, ready for the next person at the back of the line to leapfrog.

4 The game continues for as long as you like or until you run out of space. Then you can turn around and come back again!

YOU WILL NEED

At least 2 people, but the more the merrier

TOP TIP

As you get more confident, the 'obstacles' can get higher. Players can bend over rather than kneeling down, making sure to brace themselves by putting their hands on their thighs and tucking their heads right in for safety.

FRISBEE

Whether you're on the beach, at a picnic, or in your own back garden, nothing beats the versatility of the Frisbee. You can play catch with friends, fetch with the dog or teach yourself new tricks. There are hours of wrist-flicking entertainment to be had from this simple-looking object. If the standard game of throwing the Frisbee to each other starts to get a bit repetitive, there are plenty of variations you can try.

SKILL LEVEL	★ ★
TIME NEEDED	5 minutes

YOU WILL NEED

A Frisbee

At least 2 people, but more can join in

FRISBEE BOULES

Throw a tennis ball on the lawn, then take turns trying to land a Frisbee as close to it as possible. The player who gets the Frisbee nearest to the ball wins.

TRICK FRISBEE

Impress your friends by spinning a Frisbee on your finger. Simply spray a light coating of vegetable oil or silicone spray on the underside of the Frisbee. When it glides down toward you, raise your hand with your forefinger extended and just centre it under the Frisbee as it lands. It will continue to spin and amaze all onlookers.

FANCY CATCHES

Another way to look good is to do a flashy catch. A good one for novices is the flamingo. When a slow, flat throw about knee high comes your way, raise one leg high behind you and with the opposite hand behind your standing leg, catch the disc. You'll look so cool. Other tricks known to impress are catching it behind your back or while leaping in the air.

DID YOU KNOW?

The record for the longest Frisbee toss by an under 13-year-old girl is held by American Mary Uhlarik who threw it 123 metres (403.5 feet) on 30 May 1992, at Anaheim, California.

SOFTBALL

If you know how to play baseball, then you'll probably pick up softball really quickly because it too involves hitting a ball with a bat and trying to make it around all the bases. So get your swinging arm at the ready.

SKILL LEVEL	★
TIME NEEDED	1–2 hours

1 Mark out a diamond with 18 metres (60 feet) between bases and 12 metres (40 feet) from pitcher's mound to home plate.

2 Each team takes turns at batting and then defence. The aim of the team that is batting is to score as many runs as possible by getting runners around all the bases and back to the home plate.

3 A batter is out if the ball, once hit, is caught in the air; if the ball is caught and thrown at any base before a runner gets there; a runner is tagged by the ball (touched by the ball or the glove of an opposition player) while running between bases; or if three strikes are called by the umpire.

4 A strike is if the ball is pitched outside the strike zone (between batter's armpit and knee), if you swing and miss the ball or if the pitched ball hits the batter.

5 When three of your batters have been ruled out then your team is out and the other team comes in to bat.

6 When fielding, the pitcher throws the ball underhand and can only take one step forward to throw.

7 The team with the most points after seven innings is the winner. If the score is tied, extra innings are played.

YOU WILL NEED

A softball diamond or large playing area and cones

A baseball bat

A softball (slightly bigger – 30-cm (12-in) circumference – and a little softer than a baseball)

Players (officially you need 9 players per team but any even number will do)

DID YOU KNOW?

Softball was originally invented in 1887, as a winter version of the sport of baseball. It was called indoor softball until the 1920s when the name changed to softball and it became an organized sport.

BEAN-BAG TOSS

Depending on where you were born and raised, you might call this game anything from corn toss to soft horseshoes. It doesn't much matter where you play or what you call it, it's good fun for all ages and can be played anywhere.

SKILL LEVEL	★
TIME NEEDED	30 minutes

1 The bean bag platforms (wooden boxes with a large hole cut in the top) are set about 9 metres (30 feet) away from players.

2 Divide players into teams. A player from each team takes a turn to pitch his/her four bean bags at the bean bag platforms until a contestant reaches the score of 21 points. A bean bag in the hole scores three points, while one on the platform scores one point.

3 You'll be surprised at how the scoring whizzes along and how often the lead can change hands before a winner is declared.

YOU WILL NEED

2 bean bag or cornhole platforms (available from toy shops)

8 bean or corn bags

A minimum of 2 players

JUMPING ROPE

Jumping rope, or skipping as it's also called, is a great way to get in shape, and it's fun. It's one of the few games you can play on your own or with your friends and, if you have a long rope, you can even skip in groups.

SKILL LEVEL	★
TIME NEEDED	5 minutes

BASIC JUMP

1 Hold the handles of the rope in each hand with the rope behind you. Swing the rope over your head.

2 Keeping both feet together, as the rope comes down in front of you toward the ground, jump over it.

3 Repeat this 10 times or until you get tangled up, whichever comes first.

4 Once you've mastered this, you've got the basics of skipping. Now it's time to move on!

YOU WILL NEED

A jump rope or skipping rope

Bags of energy!

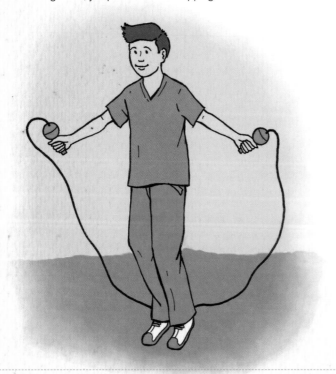

DOUBLE TURN

This one is quite an advanced trick and, to succeed, you'll need to jump high and turn the rope as fast as you can. Good luck!

1 Start with a normal, single bounce from the basic jump.

2 Then, jump high into the air and turn the rope fast so that it passes beneath your feet twice before you land.

TOP TIP

Try to land on the balls of your feet and to bend your knees on landing to absorb the shock. Keep your arms at your sides and turn the rope with your wrists, to minimize your arm movements.

FRONT STRADDLE

1 Turn the rope and jump with one foot in front and the other behind.

2 As the rope comes around again, jump again but switch the position of your legs.

FRONT CROSS

This one will really impress your friends.

1 Do a normal jump with the first turn of the rope.

2 As the rope comes around for the next turn, cross your arms in front of you and jump through the loop it makes.

3 Try switching between front cross jumps and normal jumps if you want to look like a true pro.

FRENCH SKIPPING

Success at French skipping relies on skill and agility rather than strength. Below is an example of a jump pattern but there are many routines in circulation that you can play for variation, or you can make up your own. Many of these routines are performed while chanting a rhyme. Why not ask an adult if they can remember any from their playground days?

SKILL LEVEL	★
TIME NEEDED	15 minutes

1 Get your two friends to stand opposite each other with the loop around their ankles, holding it apart with their feet at hip width.

2 You will be the jumper first. Start by standing with your feet straddling the left-hand side of the elastic. Then jump so that your feet land straddling the right-hand length of elastic.

3 Next, jump so both feet land inside the elastic loop and then jump and land with both feet outside the elastic loop.

4 Repeat step 2 and then finish by jumping and landing with both feet together to the side of the elastic.

5 If completed successfully, the height of the elastic is raised to the knees and the jump pattern repeated, then the elastic is raised to the thighs, waist and so on.

6 If you fail a jump at any level, you replace one of the players holding the elastic and then it's their turn.

7 Once you've mastered the basics, the game can be made more difficult: skinny (using only one foot to hold the elastic); wide (legs as far apart as possible); blind (jumper's eyes closed); crossover (the elastic closest to the jumper is crossed over the far elastic and the routine completed in the resulting triangle of elastic).

8 The game can also be played in teams, where, if the first jumper makes a mistake, the second jumper must then complete the routine twice.

YOU WILL NEED

A piece of sewing elastic sewn in a loop

3 or more people to play

TOP TIP

If you don't have any sewing elastic, you can link large elastic bands together to form a long loop.

JACKS

This is a game of skill that is not only fun to play, but also very useful to help you improve your hand-eye coordination. You'll find that good coordination skills can help in all manner of ways in modern life, not least in sports and video games.

SKILL LEVEL	★
TIME NEEDED	15 minutes

1 To start, throw the five jacks on the ground and then pick up the ball.

2 Now, throw the ball up in the air, and with the same hand, pick up one jack and then catch the ball before it hits the ground.

3 Put the retrieved jack in your other hand. Repeat until all the jacks have been picked up.

4 Now throw the jacks back on the floor and start again, but this time, two jacks must be picked up each time except for the final throw when, obviously, only one jack is picked up.

5 If you succeed at this round, you play again but picking up three jacks and then again with four jacks, and finally the ball is thrown up and all five jacks are picked up at once before the ball is caught.

6 If you miss the ball or don't manage to pick up the right number of jacks, your turn is over and the next player has a try. If you're playing on your own, you go back to the beginning of that round.

YOU WILL NEED

5 jacks (6-pronged and tipped with a ball on the end of each prong)

A small bouncy ball

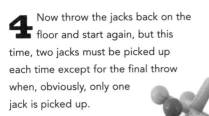

TOP TIP

In some countries, the ball is allowed to bounce once before it must be caught. This makes the game a little easier. On the other hand, if you're a real whiz at Jacks, try putting in a clap of the hands before the pickup.

5

COLD-WEATHER PLAYGROUNDS

When the autumn colours start to fade and the dark nights of winter shorten the afternoons, it's tempting to go indoors and hibernate like sleepy bears until the spring flowers start to bloom. But just because it's cold outside doesn't mean you can't enjoy the outdoors. In fact, the colder weather calls for an array of exciting activites, projects and crafts you just can't do in summer. Pretty soon, you'll be glad it's winter.

ADVENTURE PLAYGROUND

It doesn't always snow in winter, but there's still plenty of fun to be had outside. Building an adventure playground in your own back garden will give you an exciting base for all-day-long fun. Here are some suggestions for features that should be reasonably easy to construct at home.

SKILL LEVEL	★★★
TIME NEEDED	1 day

TYRE SWING Obtain a worn-out car tyre (ask at your local rubbish dump if you don't have any at hand) and a length of strong rope. Ask an adult to tie the rope securely to a low branch of an overhanging tree that's strong enough to support the weight of a full-grown person, and then secure the other end to your tyre so that it hangs at about waist height. Make sure there's plenty of room on either side for the swing to work in, and soft turf or woodchips beneath.

GROUND LOOPS Larger tyres can make another playground feature. Obtain a tractor tyre from a rubbish dump and, with help from an adult, dig a hole in the ground deep enough to hold slightly more than half the tyre when it is standing upright. Place the tyre in the hole and fill in any gaps with earth up to ground height. Pack down any rough surfaces with loose soil. You can now use the tyre to climb on and crawl through. If you have the time – and enough tyres – place three tyres side by side to make a tunnel or ridge of tyres that you can clamber through or hop across.

SANDBOX A sandbox is a classic play accessory. First, work out how large you want the sandbox to be. Then go with an adult to a hardware store and buy enough 2.5-centimetre (1-inch) thick, weather-treated hardwood planks to make the sides of the box. With the help of an adult, excavate the desired area of soil to the same depth as the planks are wide. Ask an adult to cut the planks to length with a handsaw and fit them in position, upright on their sides, pegging them in place with thick pegs of wood driven into the soil so they hold the planks in position. Then fill the box up to the brim with builder's sand.

YOU WILL NEED

Worn-out tyres

A strong rope

An overhanging tree

Tractor tyres

A shovel

Some 2.5-cm (1-in) thick weather-treated planks

A handsaw

Some thick wood pegs

Sand

Adult assistance

DRESSING-UP RACE

Polar explorers need to put on a lot of warm clothing and equipment before they can venture out onto the tundra (which is like a desert that has ice instead of sand). This race tests the ability of competitors to dress up in full gear in a hurry! It will also get everyone warmed up nicely for the other events.

SKILL LEVEL	★
TIME NEEDED	30 minutes

1 Before the race, prepare a bag of bulky outdoor clothing and items for each competitor – you can include things like parka jackets, waterproof pants, snow goggles, a furry hat, snowshoes and a backpack: in fact, the more the better – as long as each bag contains similar items. For extra entertainment value, try placing in a few silly items like pink fluffy earmuffs!

2 Place the bags in a row about 20 metres (65 feet) from the start line.

3 The aim is to see who can get all of the items on first, so when the judge blows a whistle, the competitors must race each other to their bags.

4 The first one to don all their items and shout 'Ready!' is the winner.

YOU WILL NEED

A variety of winter clothing, such as jackets, hats and shoes

MAKING A BIRD FEEDER

Birdwatching is a lot of fun, and making a bird feeder is a great way to attract a range of species to your garden. Many bird species migrate to other climates so keep an eye out for birds that can only be seen at certain times of the year. And, this pretty bird feeder is not only completely eco-friendly, but biodegradable too!

SKILL LEVEL	★★
TIME NEEDED	1 hour

1 Once you have decided where in the garden is safe to hang your bird feeder, you can then cut the string to the right length.

2 Tie the string securely around the top of your pine cone.

3 In a bowl, combine about 250 grams (2 cups) of seeds and oats.

4 Using the lollipop stick, spread peanut butter thickly over the pine cone, making sure all the surfaces are well covered and all gaps are filled.

5 Now roll the buttered pine cone in the seed and oat mixture, pressing down firmly to ensure the mixture sticks to the entire surface.

6 Using the attached string, hang the pine cone securely from a tree and enjoy watching the birds as they eat!

YOU WILL NEED

String

Scissors

A large pine cone

A small mixing bowl

Bird seed, shelled sunflower seeds, or rolled oats

A lollipop stick

Peanut butter

REMEMBER!

Birds have lots of predators, including cats, so hang the bird feeder where they can feed without danger of being caught.

MAKING A WIND CHIME

Modern wind chimes have their origins in Indian wind bells. They used to be hung on the corners of pagodas (tiered towers) with the purpose of scaring away birds and evil spirits. Later, these wind bells were introduced to China and were also hung in temples, palaces and homes. In feng shui (the Chinese practice of choosing and arranging work and living spaces to promote balance and comfort), wind chimes are used to attract good luck to the home. You can make this beautiful wind chime more generic or give it a real wintry feel with items that conjure up feelings of winter.

| SKILL LEVEL | ★ |
| TIME NEEDED | 1–2 hours |

YOU WILL NEED

Small bells

Bright beads of different shapes, sizes and materials (wood, clay, glass)

Pretty pebbles

Small winter-themed ornaments (if using)

A pair of scissors

A string or nylon thread (such as fishing line)

Clear-drying glue

A skewer or a scissor blade

A round lid from a plastic container (such as a margarine tub)

Brightly coloured yarn/wool

1 Select eight or ten items from your collections of beads, bells and pebbles, and/or winter-themed ornaments that you'd like to hang on your wind chime.

2 Cut string or nylon thread into lengths about 15 centimetres (6 inches) each.

3 Thread the string through the holes in your objects. (If you can't find shells with natural holes in them, you could ask an adult to drill small holes in them using an electric drill.)

4 For heavier items such as pebbles, wrap the string around the object several times, then rub glue on the string and pebble to hold it in place. Allow to dry.

5 Using a skewer or scissor blade, carefully poke small holes evenly around the edge of the plastic lid.

6 Pull the pieces of string through the holes and then tie a knot at each end so it can't slip back through.

7 Punch two holes in the middle of the plastic lid.

8 Loop a length of yarn through both holes and tie a knot. This is to hang your wind chime.

9 Hang your wind chime either inside a window or near a door so it can tinkle and chime as it catches the breeze.

DID YOU KNOW?

If the items on your wind chime are small, you can always hang several on each string.

NATURE COLLAGE

The next time you go on a walk, why not collect some nature specimens and trinkets that you can then use to make a stunning collage at home. Look out for things that are especially associated with autumn and winter including seasonal flowers, berries, twigs and leaves.

SKILL LEVEL	★ ★
TIME NEEDED	30 minutes–1 hour

1 A great way to set off a nature collage is to give it a natural background, instead of just plain paper. First, spread a thin layer of glue all over your construction paper or sheet of card.

2 Sprinkle with collected local sand or gravel to form a base layer. To give the collage a snow-like look, you can also sprinkle the paper with a layer of icing sugar on top.

3 Once the glue is dry, it is ready for you to start your collage.

4 Choose the objects that you want to use. Before gluing anything down, first arrange your collage on the background, to ensure you are happy with the way it looks.

5 Once you are happy with your arrangement, spread a little glue under each item and replace firmly on the card.

6 Once the glue has dried completely, attach the cord or string to the back of the collage using strong tape so that it hangs without any danger of falling.

YOU WILL NEED

Glue

Construction paper or card

Sand or gravel (optional)

Icing sugar (optional)

Collected items (leaves, twigs, dry moss, flowers, seeds, seedpods)

Cord or string, to hang

Strong tape

MAKING A WREATH

Many trees lose all their leaves in the autumn. After a brief blaze of red and gold, they stand bare as broomsticks until warmer weather brings new buds to their branches in spring. Some trees, known as evergreens, keep their leaves all year round. Evergreens often have waxy, needle-shaped leaves that help the tree to conserve water — which is why they can survive on freezing, stony mountain slopes high above green valleys below. Make a wreath of winter greenery to hang on your front door as a reminder that life continues to flourish even in the darkest part of the year.

SKILL LEVEL	★★
TIME NEEDED	1 hour

YOU WILL NEED

A wreath form

Some evergreen fronds

A pair of pruning shears

Florist's wire

Any extra decorative items you want

1 Obtain an inexpensive willow, vine or straw wreath form from a florist. This will be the frame on which you will construct your wreath of winter greenery.

2 Gather some slender, supple fronds from the tips of the branches of evergreen trees. Cedar, firs, pines, holly and juniper branches can all be used. With an adult's help, remove them carefully with pruning shears. Never remove greenery from a conservation or protected area.

3 Trim the evergreen fronds into small lengths of 15 centimetres (6 inches) or so.

4 Lay the wreath form on a table. Then begin attaching the fronds to the form by pushing the ends of the fronds into the twiggy structure of the wreath form, twisting the fronds around it where necessary.

5 Add more fronds all around the wreath form, until it forms a dense and bushy ring of greenery. Use florist's wire to secure any stray fronds.

6 Add decorations such as winter berries (make sure they're non-toxic), ribbons, bows or mock presents, binding them on with florist's wire here and there.

MAKING A SNOWMAN

There's nothing more exciting than the first snowfall of the winter: the soft white carpet that's replaced the green of your garden, the gentle fall of nature's pure white flakes and, of course, the chance to build a snowman that will be the envy of your neighbourhood. Just like sandcastles, there's a right and a wrong way to build a snowman. The first thing you need for the perfect snowman is the right kind of snow – not too fluffy, not too icy – but that all depends on what Mother Nature has in store, so you'll just have to make the best of what you have.

SKILL LEVEL	★ ★
TIME	30 minutes

1 Choose your building site – preferably somewhere clearly visible and surrounded by plenty of snow so that you have all the materials you need.

2 Weaing gloves, make a reasonably sized snowball, then roll it along the ground to pick up more snow to add to its size. Keep going until you have a ball that is 0.3–0.9 metres (1–3 feet) in diameter. This will be your snowman's lower body.

3 Repeat for the upper body and the head, although these should each be smaller in turn. Then, attach these to the top of the largest snowball so you have a large (lower body), medium (upper body), and small (head) ball. Make sure these are attached properly as there's nothing as sad as a decapitated snowman.

4 Make the nose with a carrot, eyes with pebbles or pieces of coal and a mouth with smaller pebbles. A hat and a scarf are obligatory clothing. Then stand back and enjoy the acclaim from your family and friends.

YOU WILL NEED

Plenty of snow

Gloves

A carrot

Pebbles

Pieces of coal

Assortment of old winter clothing (scarf, hat, gloves)

SNOW SCULPTURES

Snow seems almost purpose-made for people to have fun with. It is soft enough to mould into different forms but holds its shape when packed firm. This means you can use it to make amazing sculptures that will adorn your garden until the weather thaws. A snowman (see opposite page) is one of the simplest kinds of snow sculptures. But although snowmen are as much a part of winter as rosy cheeks, you needn't feel limited to this familiar design. Animals, castles and mountains are almost as easy to make, and it doesn't stop there.

SKILL LEVEL	★★★
TIME NEEDED	3 hours

1 Wait for a day when thick drifts of snow lie on the ground, and wrap up in your warm outdoor clothing.

2 Using a garden shovel, make a big heap of snow. This will be the basic resource from which you make the sculpture.

3 Decide what you want to make, then shape the snow into a rough outline. Use the shovel to carve out big shapes and a garden trowel to form smaller shapes, patting the snow down firm as you go.

4 Household objects like plastic tubs can help you mould snow into useful shapes that can be added to the design, such as blocks or columns. You can also roll snow into balls that can form the basic segments of a bigger design, such as a caterpillar. Always be careful not to build anything that might collapse on top of someone and hurt them, though.

5 Once you have built your basic design, use a pump-action spray bottle to spray it with water. This will form a thin film of ice on the surface that will allow you to carve out fine details with a spoon. Alternatively, use food dye to add splashes of colour to your piece of frozen art.

YOU WILL NEED

Plenty of snow

Warm outdoor clothing and gloves

A garden shovel

A garden trowel

Plastic tubs of different shapes and sizes

A pump-action spray bottle

Water

Food dye (optional)

MAKING AN ICICLE

Icicles can sometimes be seen hanging from the roofs of buildings in very cold climates. Icicles form in cold weather when dripping water freezes into a long, clear spindle of ice. If you want to view this fascinating natural phenomenon up close, you can try making your own. All you need to do is make a container that slowly drips water — then hang it outside on a particularly cold night.

SKILL LEVEL	★★
TIME NEEDED	30 minutes

1 First, find a suitable container. An old coffee tin is perfect.

2 Using a bradawl, carefully make two holes, one facing the other on either side of the tin, two centimetres or so below its top rim. Ask an adult for help if you find this part difficult.

3 Thread the string through both holes and then tie the ends of the string together securely to form a loop from which to hang the tin.

4 Next, take a drawing pin and carefully puncture a small hole in the base of the tin. It should be just big enough to allow water to gradually drip out.

5 Wait until a freezing night is forecast. Then fill your container with water and hang it outside at dusk. If there isn't a convenient nail on a wall to hang it from, try a low branch in the garden.

6 Visit it in the morning – a beautiful icicle should have formed beneath the tin. For a splash of extra fun, try adding food colouring to the water before hanging up the tin. With practice, you'll be able to make icicles of all colours of the rainbow.

YOU WILL NEED

An empty coffee tin

A bradawl

A 70-cm (28-in) piece of string

A tape measure

A drawing pin

A pair of scissors

Water

Food dye (optional)

DID YOU KNOW?

In the right conditions, natural icicles can grow to more than 6 metres (20 feet) in length.

MAKING SNOWSHOES

When you're out walking, it can be exhausting if the snow is deep. To stop you from sinking in your boots, you could make yourself a pair of snowshoes that will help you to cross the deeper patches. Snowshoes work by spreading your body weight over a larger area of snow, thus helping you to move more quickly without sinking with every step. Before people built snowshoes, nature provided examples. Several animals, most notably the snowshoe hare, have evolved oversized feet over the years which enable them to move more quickly through deep snow.

SKILL LEVEL	★★★
TIME NEEDED	1½–2 hours

1 Cut a length of plywood around 50–56 centimetres (20–22 inches) long and bend it around your knee to make it pliable.

2 Bend it into an arch and, carefully using your knife (get an adult to help you), scrape away the bark on the inside of the curve to make it more flexible.

3 Cut one side of both ends of the branch (diagonally), so that when held together, they rest flush against each other.

4 Hold these ends together and bind with string to form a hoop.

5 Find six short sticks and bind them in pairs at their centre.

6 Bind the three pairs of sticks across the hoop to support the foot.

7 Weave string in and around the frame and the cross-sticks to form the base of the snowshoe.

8 Tie the finished snowshoe to your walking boots with cord.

9 Then repeat steps one to eight to make one for the other foot.

YOU WILL NEED

Two lengths of soft plywood, 0.64 cm (¼ in) thick

A sharp knife

String

12 sticks

Cord or bootlaces

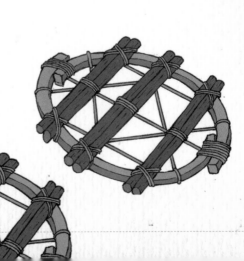

SNOW PAINTING

This activity is fun, messy and colourful, but you will need a few basic items of equipment. First, you'll need to obtain three pump-action spray bottles – the kind used to water household plants. Ask permission to use any you may already have at home, and make sure they're thoroughly rinsed out before use. Or, new spray bottles can be obtained fairly cheaply from DIY centres. You'll also need some food dyes. Green, red and blue are a good basic set of colours. Mixed with water, these will form the 'paints' that you will apply to the snow using the spray bottles.

SKILL LEVEL	★ ★
TIME NEEDED	40 minutes

1 Fill each spray bottle with water and add a small amount of a different food dye to each. Replace the tops and give it a little shake to mix the colours with the water properly.

2 Find a clean patch of snow outside and, carefully aiming the nozzle of a spray bottle, paint lines onto the snow by squirting on colour. Use the other colours you have chosen to build up a picture.

3 Using this technique, you can make simple pictures of anything from flowers to faces. You can even paint details onto a snowman (see page 94) or snow sculptures (see page 95).

YOU WILL NEED

Three pump-action spray bottles

Water

Food dyes

Snow

TOP TIPS

When buying your spray bottles, try to get transparent ones so that you can see what colour your snow paint is inside. Label the spray bottles using a permanent marker with whatever colour is in each bottle. They will keep for at least a year stored in the fridge.

Don't completely fill the bottles with water. Leave at least 2.5 centimetres (1 inch) of the bottle empty so that you can add the food colouring and still be able to put on the spray nozzle.

ICE ART

When ponds and lakes freeze over, leaves and other things are trapped in a layer of crystal-clear ice. Replicate this fascinating process by making an amazing ice mobile.

SKILL LEVEL	★★
TIME NEEDED	1 day

1 Find three shallow plastic tubs and place them on a tray. Lay a length of garden twine or wool across all three, so it rests flat on the bottom of each dish, with a little slack twine between them.

2 Place a natural object, such as a feather or plant frond, in each dish, across the twine on the bottom, and then carefully fill each dish with water.

3 If it's freezing conditions outside, leave the tray out overnight, or place it in the freezer.

4 In the morning, the water in the tubs will have frozen – encasing your natural artifacts in ice. Remove the ice mobile from the tubs and hang it up outside from the twine that links it together.

YOU WILL NEED

3 shallow plastic tubs

A tray

Some garden twine or wood

Some natural objects

1 l (4 cups) of water

BUILDING AN IGLOO

Igloos are buildings made out of snow blocks. They are the traditional homes for the Inuit people of Canada and Alaska. Some people might think the Inuit build with ice and snow because they like to be cold, but, in fact, snow has very good insulating qualities because it holds a lot of air. That means when the air outside an igloo is -40°C (-40°F), the inside of an igloo can be a toasty 16°C (60°F), even without a fire. The warmth inside an igloo comes from body heat. Building an igloo is surprisingly easy to do. You just need to have the right kind of snow and lots of it. Whenever you're sitting on cold ground or snow, your body temperature is going to drop because the ground draws the heat away. Try to sit on a raised platform or chair to stay warm inside.

SKILL LEVEL	★★★
TIME NEEDED	2–3 hours

YOU WILL NEED

A pair of waterproof, insulated gloves

Lots of dry, very hard snow

A snow shovel

A snow saw

1 Find a large supply of dry, hard snow – you want unbroken ice crystals in the snow if possible. Don't forget to wear some waterproof, insulated gloves while building your igloo.

2 Cut blocks from the snow. Get an adult to help you. Each block should be 90 centimetres (3 feet) long, 40 centimetres (15 inches) high and 20 centimetres (8 inches) deep.

3 As you cut the blocks, begin arranging them in an upwards-sloping spiral around yourself. You will be working from the inside of the dome. Shape the first block so that it slants upwards and work your way around. The hole you're making as you cut the blocks will become the floor of the igloo. Make the initial circle 2 metres (6 feet) in diameter.

4 As you build the walls up, shape each block with your snow saw so that they all slant slightly upwards and lean slightly inwards to form a dome shape. Don't worry about the front door just yet.

5 When you get near the top and there isn't any more room to stack blocks, cut a hole at ground level for the front door. It should be no more than 60 centimetres (2 feet) high.

6 Close off the top of the igloo by cutting a block of snow in the shape of the hole. Make it slightly larger than the hole. Place it on top of the igloo, then go inside and use your snow saw to cut and shape the top block.

7 Cut four more blocks and lean them teepee-fashion over the entrance tunnel. This tunnel will keep wind and snow out of the igloo and will also help funnel cold air out of it.

8 Go back inside the igloo and cut two 8-centimetre (3-inch) ventilation holes in opposite sides of the igloo dome at about waist height. This also allows cold air to escape, while the warm air gets trapped under the dome.

IGLOO VARIATIONS

If you live in an area with warm winters, you can still make your own igloo. Some people have successfully built sand igloos at the beach, but that's an inexact science where luck plays as much of a role as the building material – you need the right mix of sand and water.

If you live in the desert, you can try mud-brick igloos. The Native Americans used to create bricks out of caliche, a fine dirt found in the southwest United States. They would make a mix of mud, straw and water, pack it into brick-sized wooden moulds, and bake them in the sun for a few days.

If you can't get hold of sand or caliche, there's always a papier-mâché igloo. Make an igloo shape out of chicken wire and cover it in strips of newspaper soaked in paste made from flour and water. With a bit of white paint and a little imagination, this can make quite a cosy igloo substitute for the summer months. And unlike the snow igloo, it will never melt – until it rains!

REMEMBER!

Although it will be warmer inside the igloo than outside, you will still need to wear extra warm clothing and use a winter sleeping bag.

6

FABULOUS FEASTING

Food, glorious food! There's nothing quite as rewarding as rustling up your own snacks to share with friends and family. Learn to make your own jam, concoct homemade lemonade on hot summer days, or bake the perfect adventurer's treats, chocolate brownies and gingerbread people. Full of easy-to-follow recipes for cooking, eating and drinking, this chapter will inspire any rookie cook to feast outdoors.

PLANNING A PICNIC

Whether you're attending an outdoor concert, having a day at the beach or lake, or simply heading to your local park or out into your own back garden, eating al fresco (outdoors) is always a huge treat. So, forget the ants and wasps, pack a ball, a Frisbee or a good book, and load up your picnic hamper with some of these fun-filled picnic ideas.

SKILL LEVEL	★
TIME NEEDED	1–2 hours

Here are a few things to think about to make sure your day goes without a hitch:

SCALE: Is this picnic going to be a simple snack on the run or a fresh-air feast? Are you aiming for simplicity or to impress with gourmet dining?

GUESTS: Who do you want to invite? You've got to make sure there's enough food for everyone so think carefully about numbers and how much each person is likely to eat.

WEATHER: I know, I know… you can't change the weather, but you can take a few precautions. If it's hot, make sure your food is suitably chilled, and remember the sunscreen. If it's cloudy, a large umbrella can save the day.

NUTRITION: Picnic food should be fun but not entirely consisting of junk food, so make sure you pack some healthy food as well as treats. And don't forget something to drink.

COMFORT: No one wants to spend time sitting on wet grass or a hard rock. Pack a picnic rug or some lightweight camping chairs and you won't regret it.

FINGER FOODS: Try to choose foods that you can eat without cutlery – such as wraps – which will save on the amount you have to carry with you, and on the dish washing when you get home.

ENTERTAINMENT: Depending on your location, why not pack a ball, fishing rod or Frisbee? Or take some cord to rig up a makeshift volleyball net or limbo.

BE CREATIVE: Why not be adventurous and take a barbecue or plan a campfire picnic? How about a themed picnic where both the outfits and food have to fit the theme?

FOOD IDEAS

Well that's enough to get you thinking about what sort of picnic you'd like to plan. Now, let's get down to basics and consider the type of food you'd like to enjoy on the day.

MAIN SNACKS: A picnic doesn't just have to be about sandwiches. If you want to make your picnic a little more interesting, and avoid the problem of soggy bread, you could substitute the simple sandwich with any of the following snacks:

Tortilla wraps with a favourite filling
Wholewheat crackers
Pizza slices
Mini pittas
Bagels
Sausage rolls
Dips

VEGETABLES: You can get your vegetable quota by adding salad items to a sandwich or wrap, or pack them separately in little pots. Why not include:

Cherry tomatoes
Cucumber chunks
Carrot and celery sticks
Sticks of red or green bell pepper

FRUIT: Fruit doesn't have to be boring. Try:

Grapes, strawberries, cherries or any favourite fruit in a pot
Kiwi fruit (don't forget to take a spoon!)
Dried apricots, mixed fruits, raisins or pineapple
Ring-pull cans of fruit in juice

TREATS: Every picnic needs a sweet treat. Any of the treats in this chapter would be great, such as your own homemade oat bars, but any cakes or pastries are fine.

HOMEMADE LEMONADE

There's nothing more refreshing than homemade lemonade, and it's the perfect addition to any picnic. Once you've tasted this recipe, you'll never go back to the shop-bought stuff again!

SKILL LEVEL	★
TIME NEEDED	1 hour

1 Pour the sugar and 250 millilitres (1 cup) of the water into a saucepan. Gently bring to a boil on medium heat.

2 Once boiling, reduce to a simmer and stir until all the sugar has dissolved.

3 This syrup can now be put to one side to cool, then refrigerate for about half an hour.

4 Then mix the syrup with 1.25 millilitres (5 cups) of cold water. Add the fresh lemon juice. Mix well, serve with ice and enjoy.

YOU WILL NEED

240 g (1¼ cups) granulated sugar

1.5L (6 cups) cold water

250 ml (1 cup) freshly squeezed lemon juice (about 5–8 lemons)

A large saucepan

A jug (to serve)

ZINGY ICED TEA

If you like hot tea but fancy it with a twist, perhaps on a warm summer's day, reach for a cold, refreshing glass of iced tea.

SKILL LEVEL	★
TIME NEEDED	10 minutes

1 Bring 1.25 litres (5 cups) of water to a boil in a pan on the stove.

2 Drop in five tea bags and allow to boil for no more than a minute. Place to one side.

3 Add the sugar to a large jug. Pour in just enough hot water to melt the sugar.

4 Pour the hot tea from the pan into the pitcher, then remove the tea bags.

5 Fill the rest of the jug with ice-cold water. You can add lemon slices as a garnish if you like. Stir, serve and enjoy!

YOU WILL NEED

1.25 litres (5 cups) water

5 green tea bags (you can use black tea bags but this gives a stronger flavour)

200 g (1 cup) sugar

Iced water

Lemon slices (to garnish)

A medium-sized pan

A large jug

SUMMER SMOOTHIES

If you find it hard to eat the recommended daily portions of fruit and vegetables, we've got the perfect solution – blitz all your favourite fruits together to make a smoothie packed full of goodness. Virtually any ripe fruit you find in the fruit bowl can be used – the combinations are endless and entirely up to you. And summer is such a time of plenty for fruit that you really can go crazy. It's a good idea to use bananas as a background to other fruits because they give your finished smoothie a good, velvety texture. For a colourful smoothie, add any sort of berries, from blueberries to blackberries and mulberries.

SKILL LEVEL	★
TIME NEEDED	10 minutes

1 Add the liquid ingredients to the blender.

2 Then add the rest of the ingredients, one at a time, blitzing briefly (sometimes called pulsing) in between each new addition to avoid clogging up the blender blade.

3 Check the consistency of your smoothie. If it's too thick, add more milk; too thin, a little more yoghurt.

4 Pour into a tall glass over ice cubes, add a straw and maybe a strawberry for decoration if you like, and it's ready to drink.

YOU WILL NEED

150 ml (²/₃ cup) vanilla yoghurt

75 ml (¹/₃ cup) milk

75 ml (¹/₃ cup) orange juice

A handful of strawberries

1 banana

Strawberries (to decorate)

A handful of ice cubes

A blender

Tall glass (to serve)

MIXED BERRY JAM

You can't beat homemade jam spread thick on toast or scones. Making jam is the ideal way to preserve the taste and nutritional value of the summer fruits you've picked so that they can be enjoyed throughout the year. It also ensures that a lot of fruit will not go to waste if you have more than you can eat, and jam will last a good long time. In this simple and quick recipe, you can use any berries that are in season or that you have in the freezer. And jars of delicious homemade jam, with beautifully decorated labels, make nice gifts for your friends and family. So start saving up those old glass jars so you have plenty of containers to fill.

SKILL LEVEL	★ ★ ★
TIME NEEDED	2 days

1 Put the saucers in the freezer to chill – these will be used to test the setting point of the jam.

2 Cut the lemons in half and squeeze out the juice using a lemon juicer.

3 Place the berries, sugar and lemon juice in a large microwaveable bowl and stir until everything is well mixed.

4 Place the bowl, uncovered, in the microwave and cook on medium power for 2 minutes.

5 Remove the bowl from the microwave and stir the mixture with a wooden spoon to make sure the sugar is dissolved. Then cook for 3 more minutes, remove it, and stir again.

DID YOU KNOW?

Berry colours are caused by natural plant pigments localized mainly in berry skins and seeds. Berry pigments are usually antioxidants and berries have a very high nutrient content, making them a 'superfruit'.

YOU WILL NEED

4 tablespoons fresh lemon juice (about 2–3 lemons)

1 kg (4 cups) mixed berries (blueberries, strawberries, raspberries, blackberries)

670 g (3$\frac{1}{3}$ cups) sugar

2 saucers

A lemon juicer

A sharp knife

A large microwaveable bowl

A microwave

A ladle

A wooden spoon

Glass jars with lids (sterilized)

Labels

6 Replace the bowl in the microwave and cook on high power for about 16 minutes, removing it every 3 minutes to give it a stir, or until the jam reaches its setting point. The mixture will be very hot after heating, so be careful when stirring the mixture.

7 To check if the jam is at its setting point, take a teaspoon of the mixture and place it on a chilled saucer from the freezer. Put the saucer back in the freezer for 1 minute. Remove from the freezer and run your finger through the jam. If the mixture wrinkles and a skin forms, then the jam is ready and at its setting point. If not, continue to cook in the microwave for several minutes and then retest.

8 Once it is at its setting point, the jam can be very carefully ladled into clean jars, which should be warmed first (running them under hot water should do it).

9 Wipe any spills off the rim. Allow to cool slightly but not too much, then add the lids. If you seal while still hot, it should avoid mould growth.

10 Don't forget to stick on handwritten labels that tell you what's in the jam and the year in which you made it. Then you can store it for as long as you like.

TOP TIP

If your preserving jars do not have lids, then you can buy ready-made waxed paper tops and lids. The top goes directly onto the jam, and then the cellophane or material cover is secured on the jar using an elastic band.

PERFECT PANCAKES

In France, they're called crêpes; in America, they're eaten for breakfast; and in Britain, they're consumed in large quantities with sugar and lemon on one specific day of the year. What are we talking about? Pancakes, of course!

SKILL LEVEL	★
TIME NEEDED	45 minutes

1 In a large bowl, whisk the egg into the milk. Put the flour and salt in a mixing bowl and gradually add the milk and egg mixture, stirring vigorously all the time to remove lumps. The finished batter should be runny and have the consistency of cream.

2 Add a drop of oil to the pan and heat until hot on a high heat. Add two large spoonfuls of batter and tilt the pan until it is thinly but evenly coated.

3 The first side only takes about 1 minute to cook. When it's done, flip the pancake. Cook the other side and then place on a plate,

add the toppings of your choice, roll and enjoy!

4 If you're feeling confident, you can toss the pancake rather than just flipping it with a spatula. Shake the pan to make sure the cooked side isn't sticking to it, then swing the pan forward with a flick of the wrist. The pancake should jump out of the pan, neatly turn over, and land cooked-side-up. You might want to practise that a few times!

YOU WILL NEED

1 egg

280 ml (1¼ cups) milk

8 heaped teaspoons of plain flour

A pinch of salt

1 tablespoon of light oil such as vegetable or sunflower oil

Toppings of your choice

A large bowl

A mixing bowl

A heavy-based frying pan

Spatula

DID YOU KNOW?

The world's biggest pancake was cooked in Rochdale, Greater Manchester, England, in 1994. It was 15 metres (50 feet) in diameter, weighed 3 metric tons, and had an estimated 2 million calories.

GINGERBREAD PEOPLE

You are never too old to enjoy making and eating gingerbread people. This recipe has just the right amount of ginger to make them flavourful but not too strong. They would be great fun to make at a sleepover, but you could also pack them as an adventurer's treat! This recipe will make about twelve gingerbread people.

SKILL LEVEL	★ ★
TIME NEEDED	45 minutes–1 hour

1 Sift the flour, bicarbonate of soda and ground ginger together in a mixing bowl.

2 Chop the butter into small pieces, and rub into dry mixture to form what looks like fine breadcrumbs.

3 Add the sugar and mix together.

4 Mix the beaten egg and light corn syrup together and gradually add to the dry mixture, mixing together to form a dough.

5 On a floured surface, roll dough out to about 3 millimetres (¼ inch) thick. Using a cookie cutter, cut out as many 'people' as you can.

6 Remaining scraps can be balled together and rolled out again to cut out more 'people'.

7 Place on a lightly greased baking sheet, and bake for approximately 10 to 15 minutes or until golden brown. Ask an adult for help when using the oven.

8 When cooked, take out of the oven using oven gloves and leave on a baking sheet for a few minutes, then transfer to a cooling rack.

9 Add decorations and then leave to cool completely.

YOU WILL NEED

340 g (3½ cups) plain flour

1 teaspoon baking soda

2 ½ teaspoons ground ginger

113 g (½ cup) unsalted butter

170 g (¾ cups) light brown soft sugar

1 egg, beaten

4 tablespoons light corn syrup

Currants or small sweets (to decorate)

A mixing bowl

A sieve

A rolling pin

A gingerbread person cookie cutter

A greased baking sheet

Oven gloves

CHOCOLATE BROWNIES

This simple-to-follow recipe gives you two dozen perfect chocolate brownies – gooey on the inside, and lovely and crispy on the outside. Serve with a large dollop of your favorite ice cream and enjoy. If kept in an airtight container, you should be able to keep the brownies fresh for up to four days. If you don't trust yourself not to eat them all right away, you can always put some in the freezer for a later date.

SKILL LEVEL	★ ★
TIME NEEDED	1 hour

1 Preheat the oven to 180°C (350 °F). Grease the pan and line the base with greaseproof paper.

2 Break up the dark chocolate into pieces and place in a microwaveable bowl.

3 Heat in a microwave on medium power for 10 to 15 seconds, and then check the consistency. Keep reheating for 10 to 15 seconds until the chocolate is smooth and fully melted. Set aside to cool slightly.

4 Put the butter and sugar into a bowl and beat with electric mixer until light and fluffy.

5 Gradually add the beaten eggs, mixing well after each.

YOU WILL NEED

200 g (2¼ cup) dark chocolate

A microwave

100 g (½ cup) unsalted butter, softened

250 g (1⅓ cup) granulated sugar

4 large eggs, beaten

1 teaspoon vanilla extract

60 g (⅔ cup) plain flour

60 g (⅔ cup) cocoa powder

15 cm (6 in) square baking pan

Greaseproof paper

A microwaveable bowl

A mixing bowl

An electric mixer

A sieve

Wooden and metal spoons

6 Beat in vanilla extract, then pour the cooled, melted chocolate into the mixture and mix throughly.

7 Sift the flour and cocoa powder into the mixture, and gently fold in using a metal spoon.

8 When fully combined, spoon the mixture into the prepared pan and spread evenly.

9 Bake in the oven for about 20 to 25 minutes until firm to the touch. It should still be soft in the middle, but the top should be cracked. (The chocolate will continue to cook for a short while after it comes out of the oven.)

10 Allow to cool at least 20 minutes in the pan and then remove the brownies and place it on a cutting board, then cut into pieces.

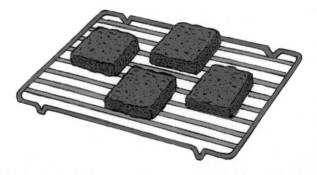

TOP TIP

Should your chocolate brownies become a bit stale, just give them a 10- second blast in the microwave and serve warm with ice cream. That should freshen them up again.

Be patient when melting chocolate in the microwave. If you zap it too long, you may burn it.

CARROT CAKE

Packed full of fruit and vegetables — yes, vegetables! — this moist cake is simply irresistible. It's quick and easy to make and tastes delicious with or without the creamy topping. Carrots have been used in sweet cakes since the Middle Ages. Back then, sweeteners were hard to come by and expensive, while carrots — which contain more sugar than any other vegetable besides the sugar beet — were much easier to get and were used to make sweet desserts. But this cake has stood the test of time, and it is still a popular dessert today.

SKILL LEVEL	★ ★
TIME NEEDED	1 hour

YOU WILL NEED

FOR THE CAKE:

1 orange

140 g ($^2/_3$ cup) butter or margarine

140 g ($^2/_3$ cup) soft brown sugar

2 large eggs

225 g (2 cups) self-raising flour

2 teaspoons baking powder (or ½ teaspoon bicarbonate of soda and 1 teaspoon cream of tartar)

100 g (1/2 cup) unsalted butter, softened

175 g (1½ cups) grated carrot

½ teaspoon vanilla extract

55 g ($^1/_3$ cup) golden raisins

Orange zester or fine grater and lemon squeezer

Mixing bowl

Wooden spoon or handheld electric mixer

Metal spoon

18 cm (7 in) square baking tin

Greaseproof paper

1 Preheat the oven to 190°C (375°F) and lightly grease a baking tin.

2 Place the tin on doubled greaseproof paper and draw around the base. Carefully cut out two layers of greaseproof paper to line.

3 Grate or zest the orange and then squeeze out its juice using a lemon squeezer. Put the zest and juice to one side while you make the cake mix.

4 In a large mixing bowl, mix the butter and sugar together until light and fluffy.

5 Add the eggs one at a time and beat in to the mixture.

DID YOU KNOW?

Even though carrots have been used in cooking as a sweetener since medieval times, it was not until the 1960s that Viola Schlicting from Texas created the first recognized carrot cake, derived from a German carrot-nut bread recipe. Now carrot cake is a firm favourite in every coffee shop and bakery.

6 Add the flour slowly and fold into the mixture using the metal spoon.

7 In the same way, fold in the baking powder (or bicarbonate of soda and cream of tartar), orange zest and juice, grated carrot, vanilla extract, and raisins. If the grated carrot is soggy, pat it dry with paper towel before adding it to the mixture.

8 When all the ingredients are well combined, scoop the mixture into the prepared tin.

9 Bake in the middle of the preheated oven for 45 to 50 minutes until the cake is golden brown.

10 Using oven gloves, carefully remove the cake from the oven and allow to cool in the pan before taking it out.

11 While the cake is cooling, you can make the icing, if you want to add this step.

12 To make the icing, put all the ingredients into a mixing bowl and blend well together until the mixture is smooth.

13 Once the cake is completely cooled, remove it from the baking tin, spread the topping thickly over the cake and serve.

YOU WILL NEED

FOR THE ICING:

210 g (1 cup) cream cheese

57 g (¼ cup) unsalted butter, softened

48 g (¼ cup) sifted icing sugar

1 teaspoon orange essence

Mixing bowl

Wooden spoon or handheld electric mixer

Oven gloves

TOP TIP

This cake will stay fresh for a few days in an airtight container – that's if you can resist it for that long!

PLUM PIE

Pie is a favourite all year round, and is easy to adjust to suit whatever fruit is currently in season. Certain varieties of plums are still in season in October and early November, when many fresh fruits have ceased to grow, which makes this plum pie a good option for autumn and winter.

SKILL LEVEL	★ ★
TIME NEEDED	3 hours

1 Preheat the oven to 200°C (400°F). Place the baking tray in the oven to heat up.

2 Thickly slice plums and place in a saucepan with sugar and ground cloves, if using.

3 Heat and simmer until the sugar dissolves and the plums are soft and juicy.

4 Put the cornstarch in a cup and spoon on some of the juice from the plums to mix it into a smooth consistency.

5 Pour the cornflour mix into the cooking fruit and mix well. Boil for a few minutes, stirring constantly until the mixture has thickened. Remove from the heat.

6 Now roll out two-thirds of the pastry on a clean, floured surface. Use to carefully line pie dish, allowing the pastry to hang over the edges a little. Press the pastry down gently into the tin.

YOU WILL NEED

FOR THE PIE CRUST:

500 g (1 lb) pack shortcrust pastry

1 egg

Flour (for dusting)

FOR THE FILLING:

900 g (4 cups) plums, with stones removed

140 g (1½ cups) brown sugar (plus a little extra for decorating)

½ teaspoon ground cloves (optional)

1 heaped tablespoon cornflour

EQUIPMENT:

A large saucepan

A rolling pin

23-cm (9-inch) pie dish

A large baking tray

A pastry brush

Wooden and metal spoons

Oven gloves

7 Pour the plum mixture into the pie. Roll out the remaining pastry until it is slightly larger than the pie dish.

8 Drape the pastry lid over the plum filling, pinching the edges together well. Using a sharp knife, cut a small cross in the middle of the pastry lid.

9 Now brush the pastry top evenly with the beaten egg and sprinkle with extra sugar.

10 Using oven gloves, place the dish on the hot baking tray. Bake for 25 to 30 minutes, until golden brown.

11 Serve your pie hot or cold, and either on its own or with a scoop of ice cream, whipped cream or custard, using the recipe below.

HOMEMADE CUSTARD

If you're feeling really ambitious, you can make your own custard to accompany your plum pie. It takes a little patience, but the results are well worth the effort.

1 In a large bowl, beat the egg yolks with the sugar.

2 Heat the milk and allow to almost come to a boil.

3 Pour the hot milk over the egg yolks, whisking hard. When completely mixed in, return to the pan.

4 Stir over a low heat until the mixture thickens enough to coat the back of the spoon. This will take about 5 to 6 minutes.

5 Remove from the heat and add the vanilla extract. Serve with your plum pie immediately.

YOU WILL NEED

2 egg yolks

1 tablespoon granulated sugar

290 ml (1¼ cups) milk

1 teaspoon vanilla extract

A large mixing bowl

A wooden spoon

A saucepan

A metal whisk

FRUIT CAKE

Lots of kids find fruit cake a bit heavy, but wait until your friends try this yummy version. It is so moist, light and packed full of fruit that they won't be able to resist coming back for another slice. And unlike traditional fruit cakes, it really is quick and easy to make. When buying the dried fruit and sugared peel for this recipe, look for the natural, unsulphured variety – it will make this cake much healthier.

SKILL LEVEL ★★

TIME NEEDED 1 hour

1 Preheat the oven to 180°C (350°F) and lightly grease the baking pan. Line the base and sides with two layers of greaseproof paper.

2 Put the butter or margarine, sugar, fruit, water, grape juice, bicarbonate of soda and mixed spice into a saucepan over moderate heat. Bring to a boil and then simmer for 1 minute.

3 Pour into a mixing bowl and allow to cool.

4 Once cooled, add eggs, flours and salt, and mix well.

5 Pour mixture into the lined tin. Bake for around 1¼ hours (if top of cake starts to brown too much, put some brown paper over the top to stop it from burning).

6 To test if the cake is ready, insert a toothpick in the middle of the cake. If it comes out clean, the cake is ready.

7 Using oven gloves, carefully remove from the tin, remove the greaseproof paper and leave to cool on a wire rack.

8 Unlike many rich fruit cakes, this delicious version is ready to eat right away. However, if you wanted to use this recipe for a Christmas cake, it is certainly special enough. Simply cover in marzipan and then ice it.

YOU WILL NEED

340 g (2 ½ cups) mixed dried fruit (including raisins, sugared peel, cherries – whatever you like)

120 ml (½ cup) white grape juice

120 ml (½ cup) water

120 g (½ cup) plain flour

120 g (½ cup) cup self-raising flour

Pinch of salt

1 teaspoon bicarbonate of soda

½ teaspoon mixed spice

120 g (½ cup) unsalted butter or margarine, softened

170 g (²/₃ cup) sugar

2 large eggs, beaten

Large saucepan

Mixing bowl

Wooden spoon or handheld electric mixer

Metal spoon

18 cm (7 in) square or 20 cm (8 in) round cake tin

Greaseproof paper

Oven gloves

TOFFEE APPLES

Nights around the campfire just wouldn't be the same without candy apples. They are always a popular treat at festivals and carnivals and are perfect for any winter parties you're throwing at home. Or, since they are fun and so simple to make, you can brighten up any gloomy winter's day by making a batch of these lovely, bright treats.

SKILL LEVEL	★ ★
TIME NEEDED	3 hours

YOU WILL NEED

6 apples (red and/or green)

225 g (1¼ cup) granulated sugar

110 ml (½ cup) water

1½ tablespoons (30 g) butter

2 tablespoons light corn syrup

Red food colouring (optional)

6 lolly sticks

A heavy-based saucepan

A baking tray

Parchment paper

1 Push the wooden lolly sticks halfway into the apples, near the stalk.

2 Place sugar and water in the saucepan and dissolve over a medium heat.

3 Add butter, syrup and food colouring (if using), and slowly bring to a boil to create toffee.

4 Allow to boil without stirring until the toffee cracks softly.

5 Remove pan from the heat and carefully dip each apple into the toffee, turning them so that they are completely coated.

6 Let them stand on a baking tray lined with parchment paper and allow to harden.

REMEMBER!

Be very careful when dipping the apples so that you don't get the hot toffee mixture on you, as it will stick to your skin and burn you.

CHICKEN SOUP

There is nothing more comforting than a bowl of nourishing homemade soup, especially on a cold winter's day. It's just what you need to stay warm and fill you with energy to keep up with your winter adventures. Soup is also very easy to make, using whatever vegetables and ingredients you have in the house, and it is also a great way to use up leftovers. To turn this recipe into a vegetarian option, simply swap the chicken and stock for two tins of canned tomatoes.

SKILL LEVEL	★
TIME NEEDED	45 minutes

1 In a large saucepan, sweat the onion in the oil on a low heat for 5 minutes.

2 Add the stock, carrots, whole chicken breast and bay leaf. Season with salt and pepper, and simmer on medium heat until the meat and vegetables are cooked thoroughly, probably for about 20 minutes.

3 Carefully remove the chicken breast from the pan and cut it into bite-sized pieces.

4 Toss half the chicken pieces back into the pan. Using a handheld mixer, blend everything until smooth.

5 Add the remaining chicken pieces, heat through again and serve with warm bread.

YOU WILL NEED

½ onion, peeled and diced

1 tablespoon oil

1 litre (4 cups) chicken stock

3 carrots, peeled and diced

1 chicken breast, left whole

Bay leaf

Salt and pepper

Large saucepan

Handheld mixer

BEEF STEW

Stew is a wonderfully warming dish. Surprisingly, it takes less than half an hour to actually prepare, and you can then let it simmer for the next two and a half hours, leaving you free to do what you want. This recipe uses beef, but originally Irish stew was made using lamb or mutton. Often, lamb or mutton trimmings were the only basis for the stock. Yet, they still held enough flavours to do justice to this hearty dish.

SKILL LEVEL	★
TIME NEEDED	2–3 hours

1 Put flour, salt and pepper and beef into a large plastic bag. Seal the top, trapping some air in the bag. Then shake to coat the meat evenly in flour.

2 Heat vegetable oil in the pan over medium-high heat.

3 Add beef to hot oil and cook, stirring regularly until browned.

4 Stir in garlic and cook, stirring for about a minute.

5 Add tomato purée, brown sugar, Worcestershire sauce, thyme and beef stock.

6 Bring to a boil, then reduce heat and simmer for one hour.

7 Add potatoes, onion and carrots, and stir.

8 Allow to cook for another hour, until vegetables and meat are tender.

9 Serve the stew in bowls with crusty bread.

YOU WILL NEED

60 g (½ cup) flour

450 g (2½ cup) cubed stewing beef

3 tablespoons vegetable or sunflower oil

2 cloves garlic, crushed

2 tablespoons tomato purée

1 tablespoon brown sugar

1 tablespoon Worcestershire sauce

2 teaspoons thyme

1.2 litres (5 cups) beef stock

6 medium-sized potatoes, peeled and cut into 2.54-cm (1-in) chunks

1 large onion, chopped

4 carrots, peeled and cut into chunks

Salt and pepper, to taste

Crusty bread (to serve)

Large plastic bag

Heavy-based large casserole dish

Metal spoon

HOT CHOCOLATE

What could be more comforting and cosy on a cold night than snuggling up with a cup of creamy, homemade hot chocolate? You can use any kind of chocolate for this recipe – you can even use chocolate chips if you have them because they melt easily. For an indulgent treat you can add toppings to your hot chocolate, such as marshmallows, whipped cream, sprinkles, grated chocolate or chocolate chips.

SKILL LEVEL   ★
TIME NEEDED   20 minutes

1 First, place the chunks of chopped chocolate into a heat-resistant bowl.

2 Bring a little water to a boil in a saucepan. Turn the heat down to a low boil and place the bowl over the saucepan so that it does not touch the bottom and fits snugly in the rim.

3 Stir the chocolate occasionally until it has all melted and has a smooth consistency.

4 Put the melted chocolate to one side while you heat the milk in a saucepan over a low heat. Keep an eye on the chocolate to make sure it doesn't harden.

5 Add the melted chocolate to the warm milk, mixing well. If you add only a little milk or water to melted chocolate, it forms a solid lump. To make sure that you get a smooth, silky hot chocolate drink rather than a lumpy mess, make sure you follow the recipe to get the right ratio of liquid to chocolate.

6 Add your chosen toppings and allow to cool slightly before sipping and enjoying your delicious hot chocolate drink.

YOU WILL NEED

170 g (²/₃ cups) chopped chocolate (plus extra for dusting)

500 ml (2 cups) milk or water

Toppings (optional)

Heat-resistant bowl

A saucepan

A wooden spoon

OAT BARS

Delicious and nutritious, these tasty bars are the perfect accompaniment for activity-filled days. Another name for them is Hudson Bay Bread, and they have their origins in scout expeditions in Canada. With this recipe, you can make the perfect oat bars for filling you up when you're in need of an energy boost

SKILL LEVEL	★ ★
TIME NEEDED	1 hour

1 Preheat the oven to 190°C (375°F).

2 Melt the butter in a small saucepan, making sure you don't let it turn brown.

3 Using sunflower oil, grease the baking tin.

4 Mix the oats, dried fruit (if you are using them) and syrup in a mixing bowl.

5 Add the sugar and the melted butter. Mix well with a wooden spoon.

6 Tip the mixture into the prepared baking tin and press it down flat with the back of the wooden spoon.

7 Using oven gloves, put the tin in the oven and bake for 25 to 30 minutes until golden and turning brown at the edges.

8 Carefully remove the tin from the oven wearing oven gloves.

9 Cut into 16 slices and leave to cool in the tin.

10 When completely cool, remove from the tin and enjoy!

YOU WILL NEED

150 g (²/₃ cup) butter

1 tablespoon sunflower oil, for greasing

200 g (2¼ cups) rolled oats

70 g (½ cup) raisins or chopped dried apricots (optional)

2 tablespoons light corn syrup

100 g (1 cup) caster sugar

A small saucepan

A mixing bowl

A wooden spoon

A shallow baking tin, 30 x 25 cm (12 x 10 in)

Oven gloves

TOP TIP

Oat bars are ideal snacks for when you are hiking on the trail because they release energy slowly.

CHOCOLATE LOG

A homemade chocolate roll dusted with icing sugar is the perfect centrepiece for a special occasion. It's a challenge to make, but once you get the hang of it, the results are well worth the effort — and if you follow these simple instructions you should have no problems. The tricky part is rolling up the cooked cake without it breaking, so be extra careful when doing that step. And remember, any minor cracks and breaks can be disguised with the icing, so don't get disheartened if it doesn't go perfectly, especially the first time.

1 Preheat the oven to 180°C (350°F) and grease the Swiss roll tin. Then line the tin with greaseproof paper.

2 Sift the flour and cocoa powder together.

3 Using an electric mixer, beat the egg whites until they are stiff, and then gradually add the granulated sugar, beating continuously until the mixture is thick and the sugar is completely dissolved.

4 Beat in the egg yolks and add the hot water.

5 Using a metal spoon, fold in the sifted flour and cocoa.

6 Pour the mixture into the prepared Swiss roll tin and bake in the oven for 12 to 15 minutes.

SKILL LEVEL	★ ★ ★
TIME NEEDED	1 hour

YOU WILL NEED

Greaseproof paper

125 g (1¼ cups) plain flour

2 tablespoons cocoa powder

3 large eggs, separated

125 g (²/₃ cups) granulated sugar (plus extra for rolling)

2 tablespoons hot water

Sifted icing sugar

Swiss roll tin

A sieve

A mixing bowl

An electric mixer

Wooden and metal spoons

Oven gloves

FOR THE FILLING:

140 g (²/₃ cup) butter, softened

280 g (2¼ cups) icing sugar

1–2 drops vanilla extract

1–2 tablespoons milk